Ain't you got a right

THE PEOPLE OF JOHNS ISLAND, SOUTH CAROLINA —
THEIR FACES, THEIR WORDS AND THEIR SONGS

recorded by Guy and Candie Carawan

photographed by Robert Yellin

music transcribed by Ethel Raim / with a preface by Alan Lomax

to the tree of life?

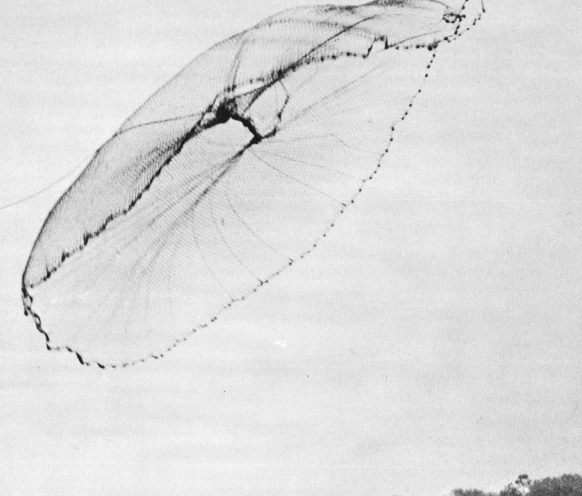

SIMON AND SCHUSTER   NEW YORK

CONTENTS

PREFACE
by Alan Lomax

AMERICA IS STILL the little-known land. Painfully striped with the lash of highways and railroads, wounded by jerry-built towns and stone jungles, the continent lies under the plane wing, still almost untouched. Away from the flat wash of neon and the sterile concrete furrows are many wayward neighborhoods where people do not merely listen and buy what they are told to buy. This is the old, dying but still green land, where talk is salty and character is cherished—the patchwork folk world of tales, songs, and rich personal communication. This book comes from the mossy edge of that world.

South of Cape Hatteras for a thousand miles along the coasts of the Carolinas and Georgia, the Atlantic Ocean quietly moves in past a string of low, flat islands, up winding tidal creeks, meeting rivers of black or brownish water. The sea islands, as they are called, form a dike of mud and sand against the waves. On them at low tide the mangrove roots are leaved with oysters and mussels, and a man can lean from his skiff and pull them off like peaches from a tree. The fisherman, flinging his net in a votive gesture, hauls up bait that will lure mullet, catfish and sea trout to his hook. Ashore, the farmer's plow breaks the loamy soil that brings in three crops of vegetables a year. Year round the great live oaks hung with Spanish moss make cool church naves of the sandy roads.

For three centuries, the population of the sea islands has been largely Negro. As slaves, they laid out and tilled the richest plantations of the old, cruel South. Many of them had been brought to the islands by Bahamian planters who moved there after slavery was abolished in the West Indies. During the Civil War, when the whites fled to the mainland, hundreds of freed Negroes joined the Union Army and formed the first Negro regiment, the 1st South Carolina Volunteers. As they drilled and worked on fortifications, they sang together. Their commanding officer, Colonel Thomas Wentworth Higginson, an ardent Abolitionist from Cambridge, Massachusetts, was deeply moved by these songs. He copied them down and printed them in the *Atlantic Monthly* in 1867. These were some of the first published notes of America's finest musical tradition; they came from the sea islands.

After the war, black soldiers rowing back home across the flats of gray waters found the ruins of plantations and took land for themselves. For three generations they lived quietly in independent Negro hamlets hidden away on the sea islands. Folk remedies healed the sick; customs and speech half-remembered from their African forebears lingered on. The earliest forms of spirituals, in which prayer, possession, music and dance were linked in their ancient African affinity, remained alive in the little "praise houses" where the islanders gathered on Sunday mornings. As in a Quaker meeting, everyone could speak . . . but not in the same quiet atmosphere, for in the sea island praise houses—as in Africa and in Negro ritual everywhere—all could and did respond when a member prayed aloud or sang. One after another the island singers, carefully trained in Negro style by their parents, added their comments and responses in melody, rhythm, and dance, pouring out rich harmonies and vibrant, complex rhythms. Today anyone may go—and should go as to a shrine—to hear this American music still growing and beautiful at its roots. For this tradition gave rise to the music which we are now proud of—the work songs, blues, jazz, and the great human statements of spirituals like "Go Down, Moses."

The lives of these people, carefully written down in their own words in this book, were hard. "I been swallerin' bitter pills and chewin' dry bones," says one old man, thinking back. They lost their bits of land to the greedy and then were forced to sell their labor to the whites for pennies. Southern poverty and Southern prejudice seeped in until these once proud fishermen-farmers and their wives found themselves a part of a segregated rural slum that stretched all the way to Texas. As the world outside touched them and disturbed their isolation, the people of Johns Island increasingly felt their poverty, their lack of education, and their helplessness. But there was one who was made restless by inequity and who was spurred to educate himself. His name is Esau

Jenkins and the last chapter of this book tells his story, set against the lives of his neighbors. He started life as a day laborer, built up a small one-man truck and bus service, moved into business, did well, and saw that he must organize his people politically. The task was long and dangerous, but today the Johns Islanders are voters, and when they come together in the community center which they built under Esau Jenkins' leadership, they begin again to feel dignity and hope.

"More light is shining," says Ben Bligen. "Can see more. Likewise you can do more and think more, 'cause I believe that more light is shining now than was shining in the past. And so help me God, I so glad that I can see some light. And I know there's more light for me. There is a bright light somewhere and I'm going to find it."

This book is a light for the South and for America. It tells the truth in a new way, for in it a whole community can be seen and heard and almost touched, and the lives and songs of many people come together to form a noble and unified statement of need and growth. Esau Jenkins, the wise leader of this island neighborhood, has found a message there for us all:

"Together let us go—sisters, brothers, blacks, whites, yellows, whatnot. We are all God's people, so we got to go together. And friends, I think all over the world today, people who love freedom are saying this morning, 'Out of Egypt I'm going to call my sons.' "

INTRODUCTION

THE PEOPLE in this book live six miles outside Charleston, South Carolina, on Johns Island, one of the sea islands that fringe the Georgia and Carolina coast. But in essence they could live in any Southern rural Negro community. They are maids, cooks, farm hands and laborers, the unemployed, people on relief, and sometimes people who should be on relief but aren't. They are the poorly educated, poverty-plagued Negroes of the South. They are not unlike many of the Negroes who marched in Selma, Alabama, and the newly awakened members of the Freedom Democratic Party in Mississippi. They are also similar to the hundreds of thousands of Negroes in the South who are still untouched by the civil rights movement.

We believe that these people—misunderstood, underestimated, neglected, virtually unknown to most Americans—have something enriching to offer us. The material in this book is a testimony to the richness of Negro folk culture and the human value to be found in a folk community.

The experiences these people relate might vary in detail from those of their counterparts elsewhere in the South, but they are representative. Their houses, their living conditions and their work are typical. The organization and style of their worship are of a pattern repeated throughout the South and often transported to the North. Variants of many of their spirituals, children's songs, folk tales, cures, and superstitions can be found in other communities. Their feelings about race relations might vary in degree from those of other communities, but the themes recur everywhere. Their strides into the future, their hopes and aspirations can be found across the South.

The Johns Island people speak with a special flavor because they have been relatively isolated from urban America. The low, flat island, covered with tidal creeks and marshes, farm land, and forests of oaks draped with gray Spanish moss, was accessible only by boat until the 1930's, when bridges and causeways connecting it with the mainland began to be built. On it live the descendants of cotton plantation slaves. Cut off from the mainland, they have retained many aspects of the old slave culture: a regional dialect—Gullah—filled with creek terms and boating phrases and still marked by distinctly African traits; a large body of folk tales, superstitions and cures; and a folk version of Christianity with a "shouting" style of singing old spirituals and a local "praise house" form of worship. Until a generation ago there were only a handful of white people on the island; today there are approximately 3,000 whites and 3,300 Negroes. Most of the Negroes are very poor and have large families and little education. They have worked for a lifetime on their own tiny bits of land and on the farms and in the kitchens of their white neighbors. Since the bridge went up, many have gone into Charleston for work, for there is little opportunity to make an adequate living on the island.

Like many communities in the South, Johns Island is in the midst of a social and cultural transition. Old and new institutions exist side by side. For people still on the folk level, Moving Star Hall—a tiny, battered clapboard building—has been the central meeting place for nearly fifty years. It houses a "tend-the-sick" and burial society, a secret fraternal order and a community of worship. Here each member can express himself freely and fully; in the Sunday night worship service each person takes his turn preaching, testifying, praying, and raising a song.

Down the road a mile or so is Wesley Methodist Church where a number of these same people attend regular Sunday services. Here the old folk ways are gradually being replaced by more formal modern practices. Wesley is a fine white wooden church with handsome brown pews, Methodist hymnals, a robed choir and an

9

organ. On the first Sunday of the month everyone listens to one preacher—the Reverend G. C. Brown who came from the mainland thirty years ago with a college degree—and the songs are led by the choir. But on the three Sundays a month when he preaches in other churches, the congregation forgets about the organ and the hymnals and sings older, unaccompanied spirituals; the service becomes much more informal and spontaneous, like that in Moving Star Hall.

Certainly the most unusual and modern institution on Johns Island is the Progressive Club, a successful consumers' cooperative owned and operated by these same people, some of the poorest on the island. It contains a large grocery store and the only gym on the island and serves as a center for adult education and voter registration. The man who conceived and organized the Progressive Club is Esau Jenkins, who was born and raised on Johns Island and is now one of the most effective grass roots leaders in the South. It was Esau who first conceived the citizenship school program which the Reverend Martin Luther King's organization now administers throughout the South. The remarkable story of Esau's life and his efforts to bring Johns Island into the present form the last chapter of this book.

WE CAME to Johns Island to learn about sea island folk life and to work with the Highlander Folk School literacy program which Esau had first suggested. Guy came first in 1959, and while helping to teach, he became the first white person to attend the all-night Christmas Watch Meeting in Moving Star Hall. What he heard there was rich and exciting; it had disappeared from most communities. He knew it was important and it brought him back year after year. In 1963 we moved with our small son into the middle of the community around Moving Star Hall. For the next two years we gradually got to know our neighbors until finally they were sharing with us many of their real treasures: their warmth, generosity, candor and humor, their wisdom, their songs and stories, the good times in their homes and fellowship in their social and religious gatherings.

During this period we worked closely with Esau Jenkins to help our friends put on a series of sea island folk festivals with some financial assistance from the Newport Folk Foundation. We also arranged for a group of singers from Moving Star Hall to travel to other parts of the country and share their songs, in an effort to keep alive some of the older folk material. For everywhere folk expression is disappearing. The old people are dying and the young are growing away from it. As Esau Jenkins says:

Now some of us, because we can read a little bit more, forget about the place we came from and some of the songs which help us go on. I remember an old woman my daddy and I helped move from a plantation where she lived and worked practically all her life. The only thing keep her going was some days she would look up at the sun and sing "Nobody Knows the Trouble I've Seen, Nobody Knows But Jesus." Other days she would sing "I Been in the Storm So Long." And when older folks sang those songs, it helped them realize they're trusting in God and reaching for a better day. We certainly wouldn't want the children to get away from it. We should cherish it, we should preserve it and keep it. . . .

Now if we hide those sweet songs and try to get away from what we came from, what will we tell our children about the achievement we have made and the distance we have come?

Perhaps the most encouraging thing that has happened in this respect during the past few years is that as the civil rights movement has reached rural people who are accustomed to folk-style church meetings, songs, and folk philosophy, the civil rights workers have had to adapt their means of communication. Fortunately this has resulted in a two-way exchange, and while rural people have begun to look to the future, to register to vote, to demand consideration, Negro leaders who had left their folk heritage behind them have begun to be moved by the fresh contact. Old songs now speak in depth of immediate problems and the message of a folk sermon is suddenly relevant. Today a main objective of civil rights workers in the Deep South is to convince rural Negroes that they do indeed have something important to offer this country.

THIS BOOK is dedicated to our friends on Johns Island. It is their book in the most real sense of the word—they speak for themselves. From them we have learned much and are learning still. Our respect and admiration are very deep, not only for the lessons of the old ways, but also for the courageous and difficult steps into the future, for the creative and persistent work of Esau Jenkins. We hope, as he does, that these friends of ours can move into their rightful place in modern America and carry with them a gift and example for us all—the many traditions of a unique American past.

*   *   *

This book is based on tape-recorded material. In putting it together we tried to use the strongest photograph to illustrate each text; the person in an accompanying photograph is not necessarily the person speaking. We have deliberately refrained from caricaturing the pronunciation of Gullah dialect by distorted spellings. The reader should have little or no difficulty with Gullah usage, particularly if he notes that "he" and "she" are often used interchangeably and that "we," "he" and "she" are often used as possessives. (For a scholarly study see Lorenzo Turner's *Africanisms in the Gullah Dialect.*)

The songs, which are transcribed here for the first time, are sung without instrumental accompaniment. In most of the religious songs, complex hand and foot rhythms are added as "the spirit" mounts. This particular style is called "shouting." All the songs can be sung in two ways: by one singer or by a group. The group versions are usually sung with an informal leader in a call and response pattern. The transcriptions are inevitably simplifications of what is sung, for to capture the subtle shadings and minute variations of pitch and rhythm would result in an almost unreadable score. Because the style is highly improvisational, the melody, the words, and the order of the verses vary with every performance and from one singer to another. Each transcription represents only one performance of a song; in some cases several variations have been included.

In an attempt to capture the improvisational style, we have used the following orthographical devices: a cue note (printed small) indicates either an alternate pitch that can be sung or the overlapping of voices where the lead-in phrase

is sung over a held note; the sign〜indicates a pronounced glissando; a grace note before a note is sung right on the beat, not before the beat; a grace note after a note is either sung right before the following note and is not so vocally prominent as the other notes (almost as if the voice were thrown back in the throat for a fraction of a second) or it indicates a drop of the voice from a vocalized pitch to nearly that of a speaking voice.

We strongly urge the reader to listen to these songs on the two records of Johns Island music that are available: *Been in the Storm So Long:* Spirituals and Shouts, Folktales and Children's Songs on Johns Island, S.C. (Folkways record FS 3842), which contains twelve of the songs in this book, and *Sea Island Folk Festival,* Moving Star Hall Singers, Johns Island, S.C. (Folkways record FS 3841), which contains another three songs and one story, in addition to material not included in this book.

The following books contain additional material on the sea islands:

W. F. Allen, C. P. Ware, L. McK. Garrison, eds., *Slave Songs of the United States*
N. G. J. Ballanta-Taylor, *St. Helena Island Spirituals*
B. A. Botkin, *Lay My Burden Down*
R. W. Gordon, chapter in *The Carolina Low Country,* compiled by the Society for the Preservation of Spirituals
Guy B. Johnson, *Folk Culture on St. Helena Island, South Carolina*
Lydia Parrish, *Slave Songs of the Georgia Sea Islands*
Elsie Clews Parsons, *Folk-lore of the Sea Islands, South Carolina*
Samuel Gaillard Stoney, *Black Genesis*

*   *   *

We would like to thank the following people and organizations: Alan Lomax for general encouragement and advice; the Newport Folk Foundation and the Highlander Research and Educational Center for generous financial assistance; Roger Phenix for help in typing recorded material; Ethel Raim for her sensitive understanding and highly skilled transcription of the music; and Robert Gottlieb and Richard Locke at Simon and Schuster for invaluable editorial help.

GUY AND CANDIE CARAWAN

11

1. BEEN IN THE STORM SO LONG

DAYS PAST

Rev. G. C. Brown

MY FATHER WAS BORN A SLAVE

My father was born a slave. He was fourteen years old before he had a shoe on his foot. And across the hills of South Carolina you could track him. They had big snows in the winter, and he wrapped his feet in gunny sacks. He said you could track him through his blood in the snow as he went out to bring the cows home during those snowy nights. In the morning he'd get up and run the cow up from where he slept all night to warm his feet, warm his hand with the warmth of their bodies. He was fourteen years old before he had his first pair of shoes.

My grandmother was half Indian. 'Course the Indians are stubborn, supposed to be. And being a half Indian and then being a slave also, she was very stubborn. She said that her master was a very cruel man. Since she was stubborn, he'd take her by the ears to the corner of a house, and just bang her head against the corner until she'd bleed. Come out covered in blood.

She died in the insane hospital in Columbia. You couldn't find three square inches on her head where there wasn't a scar when she died. And well, you find naked places all through her head where she was beaten until she be beaten into unconsciousness. Sometime she come to herself under a tree; Master had knocked her out. In her latter years it was discovered that during one of those forays the skull was crushed into her brain. The older she got, the worse it got. So she died at the age of seventy-seven, right there in Columbia Hospital. I knew her. I went to her funeral.

Mrs. Betsy Pinckney

THAT WAS THE TIME WHEN PEACE DIDN'T DECLARE

My grandmother was Hannah Seabrook. She raised me up and told me a lot about Rebel Times. Old Hannah Seabrook was a cooker and a washer. Her first husband got sold. Yes sir! They sell my father's daddy. Sell him for money.

When my father was coming up he used to have to go see what old Master wanted him to do. He was just a boy and couldn't do none of that heavy work. So the old Master would have him shine he shoes. One day he found some finger marks on 'em and knock my father down the stairs. Good thing I wasn't living in those days—you would of had to kill me first. But that was in the time when peace didn't declare.

When the war came through, my daddy, Cyrus Jenkins, was just a young boy. That time he was in the creek—had to dig the mud and mud the field for what they gonna plant that year. My daddy just up and ran off with the Yankees. He followed the Yankee until peace declared. My grandma didn't see him for four years. When he come back Grandma went to the depot. When she see her one son she drop her little bit of clothes and bind the son. That's right, had only one raggedy soldier coat and nothing else but that.

Mrs. Betsy Pinckney

SHE TAKE THE SCRAP AND MAKE
A LITTLE DRESS FOR ME

I born in 1878, the twentieth day of November. I was my ma's seventh child. Everybody run for give me name. I grow up in the white people house. I do the small things—I could thread needle for grandma, man. And they make me a little dress, you know. I even wash the Missus' feet. That's right, sir! That's right! Wash her feet in the basin. And when she was the only dressmaker 'round the village, she take the scrap and make a little dress for me.

My grandma had a scarf handkerchief—a white handkerchief she brought from Rebel Time, and when she died I tie he head with that. That's right. Yes ma'am!

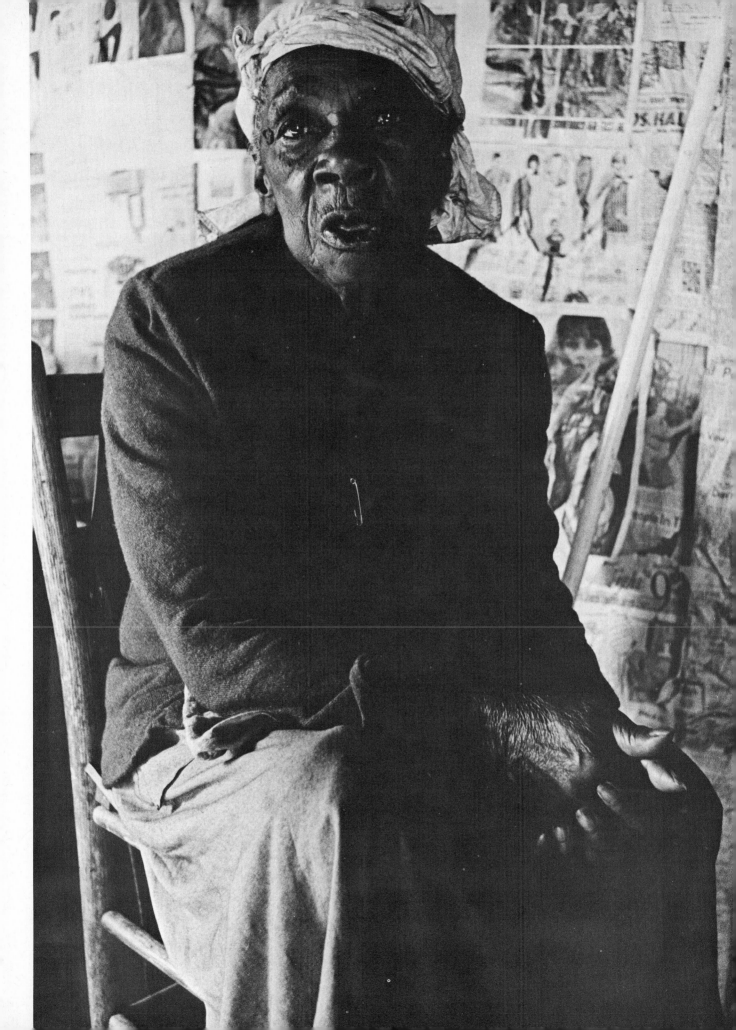

Mrs. Belle Green
WE ALL TWO WORK

I in my seventy-two. Then on the twenty-seven day of next year in August coming, I'll turn seventy-three years old.

When I married to Levy Green I was young. Me and him was married two years when the 1911 storm come. We raised on Johns Island—Levy home at Burden, the Clemmens' plantation, and my home is miles go down on that side. We didn't raise no children. I ain't got anybody. All my people dead out.

We all two work. I does work on the farm, in the field. Hoe work. Cabbage and white potato. We get three dollars a week. After I come down here I start to work with one man, and then I get so unpleasant and unfeeblish, he tell me, "If you can't work, I wouldn't look for you to work." I just give up. So painful old people now.

Levy used to work all about on the farm. He would take care of me if it the last thing he would do. Bus used to carry him all about to work. Then after he couldn't work no more, he give up. They put him on, you know—help. Wasn't much, but yet they put him on and we live by that. All of that done gone through. But I is a person don't complain. If I have anything I don't complain; if I have nothing I don't complain. It's no use. I just go on what God give me.

I thought I would done gone before Levy, 'cause I was the sickest one all the year through, but you see God took him and left me. Levy say, "Anna, don't you worry at all 'cause I going where Jesus is. Don't tell none I going, but I just go walk out."

I say, "Man, walk out where? Where you going?"

"I ain't going stay here no longer. You best try to go to the store and see if you can get something for your Christmas, 'cause I ain't go be here."

I say, "Man, hush your mouth; you talk like you don't know what you say."

He say, "I know what I say. By next Sunday I gone."

I say, "You can't know that. God only one know that."

He say, "All right then, you'll see." And he did so too. He died the fourth Sunday December, 1963.

I didn't know how old he is, but he tell me before he died, "I was born in 1880, December the twelve day." He live to be eighty-three. He was a good little man. Good little man. I have to say so 'cause I know. I sure miss him. He was all I had in the world.

Mrs. Janie Hunter

THIS WAS A KINDA POOR COUNTRY

There were ten children in my family. Daddy was a foreman for Mr. Jenkins, and he have his own garden. I work in it. All work in it. Pick lima beans, pick cotton, tie the two cotton pod in the bag, and put a string on 'em, and hang the bag around your neck, and go to each one of those cotton bush, and pick the cotton, and stuff 'em in the bag. They was paying two cents a pound. Make thirty-five or forty cents a day. Man is getting forty cents a day.

We wasn't making enough to afford a good living. My daddy, he make a living out the creek. He catch fish and we go around and sells 'em—a whole string for ten cents. Me and my sister Florence, we goes around with white dishpan on we head and sometime make two dollars. And two dollars would give you a box of food that time, 'cause food was very cheap. You could buy three cent worth of sugar, and you get a whole big piece of fat meat like that for a dime. You get a sack of grits for about fifty cent. Food was much cheaper than it is now. That's how we make living. Plant plenty of sweet potato, plenty peas and corn, and raise hog.

Then we had flat flour. That's when President Hoover had chair. We had to go 'round to Mr. Walpool yard. They used to haul the flour there in one those big van truck, and load up his barn with this flour. Then all the colored and white had to line up and call by name, and they give you a bag of flat flour. 'Til we finally made a song out of it:

What more could Mister Hoover do? What more could he do for you? He give you a sack of flour, No lard, neither baking powder, What more could he do for you?

Everybody so hungry, so want the flour. We have to mix the flour, didn't have no grease, no lard. Just put 'em in the pan and bake. Some people could afford to buy baking powder and fix it good. But who couldn't, just had to bake it—sprinkle some flour on the bottom of the frying pan so it won't stick.

But after he turned out and President Roosevelt took seat, then we began to live a little better life. I don't think just the Negro was glad; I guess some of the white too was glad when President Roosevelt took the chair. This was a kinda poor country.

Rev. G. C. Brown
THOSE WERE ROUGH DAYS

My wife and I've been here since '36. No pastor had lived here the last forty years before we came. And of course by not living with the people, they couldn't know their need and their desire. They wanted somebody to come and live with the people—that's why we came.

The first thing I found here was extreme poverty. That was during the days of the Depression, and there was no work except the WPA project. That white schoolhouse out there was built as a WPA project. The men on the farms were working for seven cents an hour. Oh yeah, seven cents. And the women, five cents.

The men plowed; the women did all the farm work. That time they didn't have planters to plant the potatoes. They cut the potatoes, dropped them in the field, and the men did all the work with the plows. That give pretty good farm employment. You had a number of men running plows, the women go along and drop the potatoes, and that give them a good day's work—several days' work in springtime. That give them employment during the planting season.

And the cabbage plant out by hand. Nowadays some have a planter. Some children worked then, but they didn't have too many children that time. There hadn't been so much marrying and going on.

Those were rough days. Food was short, scarce, didn't have much. The most they ate those days, they ate rice, grits and canned tomatoes. They bought their tomatoes at the store. They were cheap then. They bought the grits. Some made their own grits. They had a few mill. And they used to raise their own rice. There were a lot of rice farms around. They had a way of cleaning it and milling it.

Most of 'em were poor. Had no income. Very little income. They lived out of the creek. In the summertime they had crabs and shrimp, and in the wintertime had oysters. You could buy right at your door about three times a week, undressed shrimp—five cents a plate. In the wintertime we buy

fish. People went into the streams and they hauled out fish trying to make a living. Anything they could do to make a living.

They used to gather moss—this same moss. Every month a man came along with a big truck to pick up this moss for mattress factory. They had pretty good moss business. They had three or four sales a year. They had a special way to cure the moss. Dig a hole in the ground and put hot water on it and that'd make it cure quicker.

The homes were poor. Lots of the homes were built out of logs. They go into the woods and cut a log about six feet, then put another six feet. And the frame was cut out of the woods, most of it. Sills, uprights, everything—cut right out of the natural woods. And for a long time they'd be lined with newspapers and any number of houses burned down during the winter. You know those were hard days.

The chimney was built out of stick and mud. They built the frame from the ground up out of wood, and they took pine straw and mud and daub that inside and out. Kind of clay-like. They build up this fireplace and give it a shape—outside and inside. Then they make a fire and bake it. It get kind of hard like brick-making, and they'd use those for heating. That was a common thing here then. They could put a rock or something down and cook in the fireplace.

Then in the summertime most of 'em cook outdoors. They'd lay two green logs together and make a fire between and put those pots on. That was the cooking utensils.

Sometimes a rain would come, wash out a piece of the chimney in three places. It was dangerous. Sometimes a house catch afire and burn down from the chimney. Pine straw was the binder with the clay. I don't think there's one around this island anywhere now. It's been years since I've seen one.

When I came all these roads were dirt. I think that there were only three cars in my churchyard except mine. That was the general thing all over the island. They used carts and that little tacky—pony, little horse, you know. Almost everybody had a pony, marsh tacky they call it.

Rev. G. C. Brown

WORLD WAR NUMBER TWO IS WHAT CHANGED THIS ISLAND FINANCIALLY

World War Number Two is what changed this island financially. The army came and got the men, carry 'em to war. Well, the farmer had to change his plan of farm. He had to go to tractors—didn't have the manpower, see? That's when the farming situation changed; they built these roads, and they began to produce more food for defense. White farmers. Negroes have come to tractors in later years, after they got on their feet. But they have small farms. No comparison with white farms.

There weren't too many white people here then, but they owned most of the land and they had the farms. The Negroes were little farmers. Many of them had their own lots, but weren't able to build a house. World War II came, they were able to make some money and they moved off the farms and built little homes.

More people work in the city now. Nothing here to do except a few farmers to work for. Few women have employment on the farm. They work in the city as domestics. You find a few on the farm here and there. In the springtime they take trucks around and pick up the hands for the day.

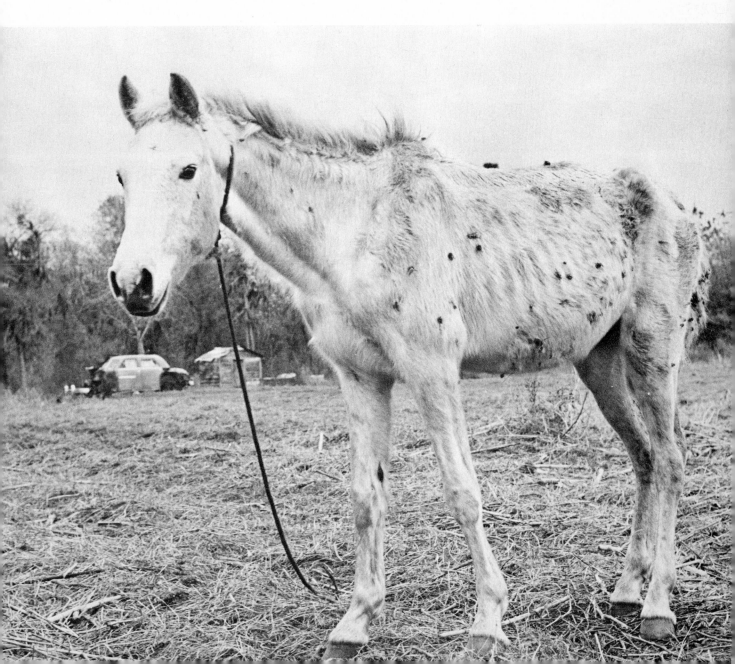

Mrs. Alice Wine
WE DO EVERYTHING FOR WESELF

Old times we never buy food. Man, you *never* used to buy nothing that time. Money use to never worry people but pay church and buy little things what you want or something like that. People raise the apple, they raise the fig tree, raise the plum, all kind of different thing. But now you got to see money. Money! You got to go for make money to buy. Is harder now. You got to work so hard to get a little bit of money. In that time you could get a quart of grits for two cents.

My daddy farm for heself. He raise he own food. We raise all vegetables. Something to keep in the barn in the winter. He plant corn, plant peas. He have sons plow. I do some too. And after we do all that, then they harvest 'em there in the barn. Then you ain't have to work in the winter.

Them times just a couple of stores, but you have to walk over seven miles to it. They sell food, but when you can plant your own, you make your own living. We have plenty chicken and have eggs and have plenty cows and have the milk. And my mother made butter—we own butter. Have we own churn and everything. Do everything for weself. So we never buy.

Those times people raise the tomatoes and the okra and can it. And they do that right now. They can it, they fix the bean, they dry the beans and the peas. They cut up the okra and they dry that.

My mother didn't never buy no kind of food. They make soap. They make plenty soap. But what they make it out, I don't know. They grind corn and make flour and grits. And we have the mortar and beat the rice. And meat, we kill the hog and put 'em in salt. End of the year, they put up hog. Kill the cow and have beef meat.

Daddy go in the creek and get we tub of fish—plenty fish that time. Get the fish out the creek—oshters, crab, mushel. Then we use to get them cookies five for a penny. Now cost penny a piece.

For clothes my daddy and mother they buy the cloth and make it. My mother had a machine and he do all his sewing.

Mr. Joe Deas

WE BEEN CLIMBING ON THE ROUGH SIDE
OF THE MOUNTAIN

From the time I have sense enough to recollect in this world, we have trouble and crosses, ups and downs. We been climbing on the rough side of the mountain—climbing up, falling back, grabbin' bottom.

Way back yonder, in 1893, we had to work for something to eat. Work on the white folks' farm, move from place to place, eat with stick for spoon. Got oshter, fish, crab and 'tato. Get corn meal, carry 'em to the mill and grind 'em and eat corn meal. Sweet potato. All that just to bring us this far. And I say thank God that I live to see light come into the world. Wise man from all part of the world come into *this* world. The world is lifting up more and more.

My old parents didn't see these things—automobile, airplane. We come from rowboat time. Had to row from home to town and back. Sometime I have to stay a whole day; have to wait on the tide, all that to row. And God spare us live to see this day.

We used to drive with ox and cart, haul wood with old oxen, plow with oxen. All that. Today no oxen. Nothing but car and truck and bus and trailer and all kind of thing like that.

Old days you couldn't eat nothing but 'tato and peas and corn and corn flour and crab and all like them. Well these days it's Christmas every day. Anything you want now you get 'em. In them days back, if one somebody kill a hog in the community, you think it was Christmas by the hog only. But now, eat hog meat any day you want. Go from store to store to get the thing you want. It's Christmas every day now for we. Light come into the world. Them times we had to buy, and money was so little, you can't see your way to buy what you need for live. Had to make out 'til we leave the white folks' place and then start to come up.

It's a blessing we see the day. Everybody lifting up. God put a way to your brains to catch on to these things, that you may have bread to carry you 'til He ready for you. The world is comin' up and is wise and wise and wise, until we *all* can get some bread from God. Man ain't able to give 'em, God put 'em into that man that he can share around to the next brother.

The Bligen Family
ROW, MICHAEL, ROW

Row, Mich-ael, row, Hal-le - lu - ion. (Oh,_____)

Row, Mich-ael, row, Hal-le - lu - ion. (Oh.)

ALTERNATE VERSION

Jump in the jol - ly boat, Hal - le - lu - ion._____ Oh,

Jump in the jol - ly boat,_ Hal - le - lu - ion._____

LEADER: Let's row the boat ashore,
GROUP: Halleluion.
LEADER: Let's row the boat ashore,
GROUP: Halleluion.

Oh see how we do row . . . etc.

Row, Michael, row . . . etc.

Let's row the boat ashore . . . etc.

Just gimme a living chance . . . etc.

Sister Mary, row your boat . . . etc.

Everybody try their chance . . . etc.

Row, Michael, row,
Halleluion.
Row, Michael, row,
Halleluion.

Mrs. Janie Hunter

ASH CAKE IS SOMETHING YOU BAKE
IN THE CHIMBLEY

Way back yonder the old lady and them had some hard times. Had to take water out the creek to cook with. They'd cook ash cake. Ash cake is something you bake in the chimbley—in the fire hearth. You have the fire hot and burn down to ashes. You mix the corn meal and you open the ashes and place the corn meal in the ashes. You haul the coals on it, and it come to a brown. After you take 'em off the hearth, you wash 'em in something call dishpan and you put it on the table and let it cold. Cut it open with the knife, and you call that ash cake.

In the old time you couldn't afford to buy coffee or tea. We'd take the corn off the cob, break the corn off the stalk and put it in the chimbley hearth and let it burn. You have a pot of water on the fire, and when the corn burn you drop it in the pot and that turn coffee. You drink that along with ash cake. For tea, you take grits and put a frying pan on the fire, let the grits parch 'til brown. Then you pour water in the pan and that turn tea. Call 'em grits tea.

Yeah boy, we come through a great tribulation. But there's freedom now. You can get anything you want if you got the money.

Mr. Willie Hunter

WE SEE MEAT, BUT WE DON'T GET IT

My aunty raised me from a little baby, 'cause I ain't know my mother, neither father. He raise me up on his farm, was plant cotton, and peas, potatoes, and all. For dinner we eat peas and some corn grits, little sweet potato, and drink some water. And after that we go back in the field, pick some more cotton, dig some more 'tato. We see meat, but we don't get it. They had little meat in the soup, you know, boil with the peas or turnip, and cook with some meat in it, but you don't get none for we children, 'cause wouldn't have that much meat for give we, understand?

Mrs. Betsy Pinckney
DON'T LET THE RAIN CATCH YOU

I remember in 1907 we had a tornado on Saxby place. I stand in my door, and my grandma say, "I going now." And I say, "Yes'm, Grandma, I see you going. Don't let the rain catch you." And you know, the wind pick up the house, just as natural as that. And it carry 'em about two tasks [a task is twenty-one rows in a field]. And my grandma lay down on the stomach and hold on to the wire fence, to the post. Yessir, I know that! And I there home whooping and hollering, "Oh Lord, that big air cloud carry Grandma!" That's right!

We had another storm in 1911. I cook peas and rice that day. It was a Sunday. Josh was laying 'cross the bed sleeping. I lean against that post and every time I feel that house shake, I say "Josh, get up. You better get up and see he going to storm." You see, I had seen one. Done gone 'cross one in 1886.

Rev. U. L. Brewer
I BEEN SWALLERIN' BITTER PILLS

I been swallerin' bitter pills and chewin' dry bones. In the old days they just give me cornbread and sweet potatoes, but still I could plow the hell out of their mules.

Mrs. Isabel Simmons
THAT'S THE WAY I COME UP IN THIS WORLD

I come up in a hard time, and I still having a hard time. I was the oldest one in the house, and I had all the work to do. When I was small they put me to tend corn—ten cents per task. Some day I do five task, some day I do six. Tend 'em. If there's two stalks in a hill you kill one off. In September we go and pick some weeds we call Morning Glory.

Sometime I use to have time to play on Sunday evening, but I couldn't go no place. I couldn't go no further than the house. I get cornstalk and make corncob dolly and play with dirt and spoon. I never went to no dance. My mother didn't allow us to leave the house. When they do have something like the Fourth of July or Labor Days, a big drum come from the city. Play drums and horn.

That's the way I come up in this world.

Mr. James Mackey
WE IS HAD A DANCE

Dance! That's my favorite. In certain times of the year like Fourth of July or Labor Days, we is had a dance. Had guitar and all like that. First of all we used something called accordion, and we'd beat stick. Then after that we was enabled enough to buy something call tambourine. A man lived back in the woods used to play guitar. James White used to play fiddle. And another fellow and I used to assist him. When I don't feel like play awhile, I dance in on the set until it broke up. We didn't have this new style they got here now—hug together.

We dance eight in a group. Two on the head this side, two on that side, two on the side like that. The fellow who knock the tambourine, he teach the set. He says "swing to your left," then you come swing that. Then swing your partner, then swing home. Then he say "promenade all," they all hook hands, grab hands together and just soshay all around, 'til they get back to the place what they was.

Later on after these girls used to come from the city, then they used to dance hug together.

Mrs. Janie Hunter

WE DIDN'T 'LOW TO GO OUT AFTER DARK

When I was a young girl, we just used to go talk with friends, we didn't 'low to go out after dark. So the first time I went to a dance—that was 1932 when I first met my husband which is Willie Hunter—my mother tell 'em to have me back in the house by sundown. He took me to a dance at Miller Hill, right over there where that water hole at. Mr. Charles Clemmens used to have a dance call a trap dance. It be drums and be washboard and all such music like that.

Used to have dances called Charleston, Pick Cherry, Alligator—get down on floor and do 'gator tap-tap, tap on your heel and toe—"One-Cent Herring, Two-Cent Grits." Sometime two hook hand and go around. Call that a waltz dance. Some of these dance now is old-time dance, but they just change and give it a different name.

Hon-ey and a one-cent her-ring, _____ And a two-cent grits, (Hon-ey) And a child like that _____ Can't do like this._ _____ Oh ray back Sam, Oh go on gal.

So when we get to the dance, the dance music was so good that we stays until about nine-thirty, and the water come across the road. The water come so high and I get scared. He have to put me on his back and tote me across the water. When we get back to the house, my mother smoke a pipe.

I was scared to go in. I said, "Willie, you best go in, 'cause I ain't going get a beating." My mother won't lick you before company.

So he went in, he says, "Mama, I'm sorry because we late. The tide was high across the road."

And my daddy, he is the first one to give in. He said, "Well, I know 'cause I go to the creek, and I know how that tide run."

I didn't say "good night." I sloop right in my bed. I was seventeen then.

Mrs. Betsy Pinckney
YOU GOT TO WORK LIKE THE DEVIL

Oh Jesus, that hoe! When I married to Josh, I couldn't lift the ground. Didn't know nothing 'bout lift ground. Josh, he work in the field. Milk the cow, then plow, man, plow. Sometime he dig the bed so wide if you reach your hoe, you better have a good long hoe stick.

We used to work for our rent and our food. You got to work like the Devil! Plant your cotton. Plant your corn. You have to work five task for that land and that house. Take oxen and plow. You have to work that 'fore you work your crop. That's you house. That's the rent. If he calls every week, you'll have to go.

In 1918 we move to our own place, where I am now. Josh go in the road and cut all them bush. Work with the ax and hoe. Some people carry the ax, some carry the hoe. Chop them bush. Cleared out the way for the cart and buggy come down. Then we had a crowd of children in there. And we had 'tato. When you throw 'em on the ground, just like somebody throwing dice on the floor. I had eleven head of children. And every one of my children had children. With the grands and the great-grands I have a hundred and forty-odd.

Mr. Willie Hunter
WE RAISE GOOD THAT TIME

I was raised right around here. Know the Bligens long before I ever marry they daughter. I know Bligen long time. My wife. All nice people. If they weren't nice people, I don't go in their family, I be in some other family. Nice people, man.

They like me too. 'Cause I have plenty manners to them. Course I raise up that way, 'cause I raise up through the old school. Plenty manners. You had to have manners to them old people that time, 'cause in that time anybody could of lick you, you been sassy with any people. But now, we don't do that.

See if anybody lick me, outside my aunt what raise me, if I go home and tell Auntie that somebody lick me, I get some *more* lick. The best thing I do, keep my mouth shut and take what I get. Oh we raise good that time. Now things changed a whole lot. But I try to raise my children like I was raised.

40

Mrs. Betsy Pinckney

EACH LEAF ON THIS TREE WILL
HEAL A NATION

I sick one time, in 1894. I sick 'til my mother and father give me up. Typhoid fever, gracious God! Oh that's a good God. I can prove it!

I was to go into the hospital the next day. There was a door, just like I looking on it now. I see a white man come through and walk just past my bed. He come and just look at me. Didn't say nothing, then go out. 1894.

And when the day was clean, the white gentleman come through the door again; I didn't know how he come in the house, but there he was. And he had on a blue gown, and hair drop on he shoulder. Yes sir! And he come to my bed, ask me, "What will you have me to do?"

And you know what I tell him? I say, "Please sir, could you read the fifteenth chapter and the psalm, 'The Lord Is My Shepherd'?"

He say, "Have you a prayer book?" Ask me just like I asking you a question!

I say, "Yes, sir."

He read the fifteenth chapter, the first six verse. Then after he done read that, he turn to the Twenty-Third Psalm, and he read it for me.

And he take me and he carry me down to a river. My spirit go on down to the river. Jesus! And when I get there, he said, "This tree bears twelve manna fruit. Every leaf on this tree will heal a nation." Gracious God have mercy!

Well sir, I wake up. I ain't seen when the man gone, but I know he come and carry me to that tree, down to that river side, and he tell me, "Each leaf on this tree will heal a nation."

Never sick so again yet! And that's the truth. Gracious God have mercy! Don't tell me don't serve God, because I going serve God until he say "well done." Yes ma'am, "well done."

Mrs. Janie Hunter

THEY WORKED THEIR OWN REMEDY

We doesn't go to no doctor. My daddy used to cook medicine—herbs medicine: seamuckle, pine top, lison molasses, shoemaker root, ground moss, peachtree leaf, big-root, bloodroot, red oak bark, terrywuk.

Now when my children have fever I boil lison molasses; squeeze little lemon juice in it. Once they go to bed it strike that fever right away. That something very good.

And you hear about children have worm? We get something call jimsey weed. You put it in a cloth and beat it. And when you done beat it, you squeeze the juice out of it, and you put four, five drop of turpentine in it, give children that to drink. You give a dose of castor oil behind 'em. You don't have to take 'em to no doctor.

If anybody fall down and break bone, my daddy get a towel and pour some water in the basin—put half a bottle of white vinegar in it. He hot the towel and bathe the leg in some mud. Go in the creek and get some mud, band that whole leg up in mud. Couple days you be walking. That knits it right back together.

For a cut, to stop 'em from bleeding, Daddy just get a big spoonful of sugar and throw 'em in there. He say once a cut stop bleeding it's not dangerous. Spider webs grow up in the house and you get that and tie 'em on. Web grow right in there.

If you get sores you get something you call St. John out in the field. And you see those little bump grow on a gum tree; you get them and you burn them two together and just tie 'em right on that wound. That heals right up.

When my little boy got a nail stuck in his feet, I got a basin of hot water with physic salt and let him hold he feet down in that—draw the poison out. Then I tie a piece of butts meat on it. His foot get better.

You hear about some little thing run back in its hole—fiddler crab? We use that for whooping cough. Catch the crab, boil 'em up with something else—I can't 'call the name—and strain 'em through a white cloth. Give that for drink. It'll cure the running whoop.

All this from old people time when they hardly been any doctor. People couldn't afford doctor, so they had to have and guess. Those old people dead out now, but they worked their own remedy and their own remedy come out good.

Mrs. Belle Green

ALL MY OWN GONE

Sometime I stand here in the nighttime, ain't but me in one little room to sing. Then I study, you know, my mind run across, and he run on the old man. I just stop, sit down, and me heart get full. The other day I couldn't eat no supper. Me heart fill, and I feel full up the whole afternoon. Couldn't do nothing. I just maybe could of get a little bit wood then.

Now I can't testify like I used to. 'Cause I ain't able. My heart been bad for so long. I just trying to hold up. But they know me; all they at Moving Star Hall know me. I full of fire too. I been way down, but the Lord lift me up. Make me feel good the week out. I just pray to make my voice come back. Give me my voice back as I does been, one time before I die.

When you get an old woman, and you can't go, the government take care of you. That's what got me today. Government got me.

Threescore and ten, that's seventy years I come to this day, but I ain't got much more. So I'm trying to be as close to the Man as I can now. But thousands and thousands have gone. All my own gone. Just a branch now, like a tree put out branch.

Mrs. Bertha Smith and
the Moving Star Hall congregation
LAY DOWN BODY

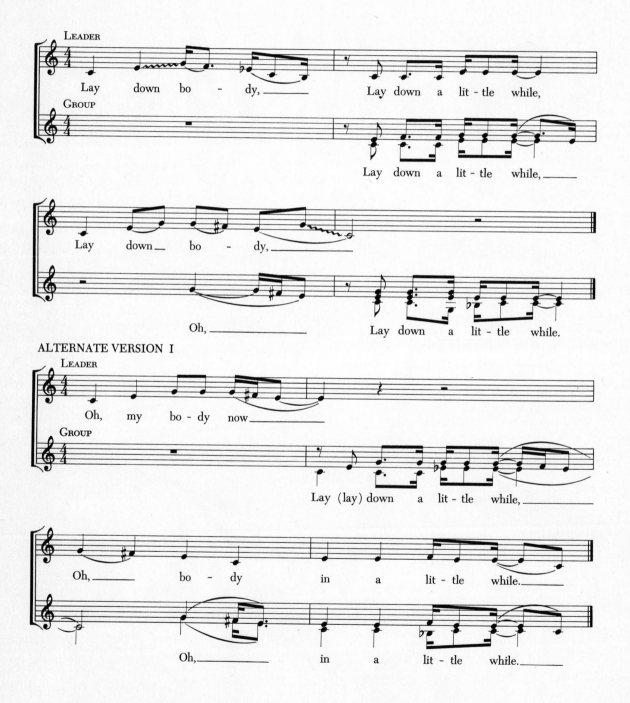

ALTERNATE VERSION I

48

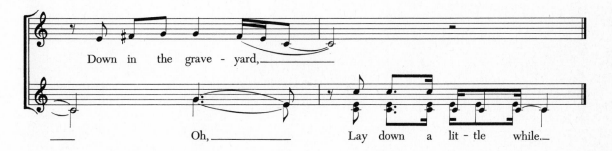

LEADER: I know you tired,
GROUP: Lay down a little while,
LEADER: I know you tired,
GROUP: Lay down a little while.

Come from a distance . . . etc.

Oh body now . . . etc.

Ain't you had a hard time? . . . etc.

Last December . . . etc.

Tedious was my journey . . . etc.

Rocky was my road, Lord . . . etc.

Ain't you got somebody gone? . . . etc.

I got somebody gone . . . etc.

Oh my body now . . . etc.

Just keep a-rollin' . . . etc.

Body, ain't you tired? . . . etc.

Body, ain't you lonesome? . . . etc.

Body, ain't you weary? . . . etc.

Lay down body,
Lay down a little while,
Lay down body,
Lay down a little while.

Mrs. Mary Pinckney

BEEN IN THE STORM SO LONG

I've _____ been in _____ the storm _____ so long _____ You know I've

been in _____ the storm _____ so long _____ Sing – in' Oh Lord _____

give me more time _____ to pray _____ I've been in _____ the storm _____ so _____ long. _____

[The following melody is most often used for additional verses.]

I am _____ a moth – er – less child, _____ Sing – in' I am _____ a moth – er – less

child, _____ Sing – in' Oh Lord, _____ give me more time _____ to pray, _____ I've

been in _____ the storm _____ so long. _____

This is a needy time,
This is a needy time,
Singin' Oh Lord, give me more time to pray,
I've been in the storm so long.

Lord, I need you now . . . etc.

Lord, I need your prayer . . . etc.

Stop this wicked race . . . etc.

Stop all my wicked ways . . . etc.

Somebody need you now . . . etc.

My neighbors need you now . . . etc.

My children need you now . . . etc.

Just look what a shape I'm in,
Just look what a shape I'm in,
Cryin' Oh Lord, give me more time to pray,
I've been in the storm so long.

51

2. THE STORM

THE PRESENT

IS PASSING OVER

Mr. Esau Jenkins

SOMETIMES WE UNDERESTIMATE THESE PEOPLE

The people on Johns Island, those that are not working in the city or as domestics, most of them make their living off truck farms on the island. Especially the women. They work on the farms of plantation owners. They pick snap beans, they dig white potatoes, they pick tomatoes, pack cabbages, spinach and whatnot. Those are the things that they depend on for a living.

During the winter months they go into a hardship because most of the farms don't have anything to do. That's the hardest time that they have to face.

Sometimes we underestimate these people and forget they have something we really need. These are people who haven't gotten a college education, or even a high school education. But anyone able to raise twelve children—and raise 'em healthy too—must know something good. They were smart enough to plant and to raise the kind of thing the children need. They raised their own hogs, they raised their cows, they had the milk with vitamin D what they need.

Some of these older people thought very deeply. Mother-wit and faith in God helped them to do a lot, and some achieved more than some of the young people who have been able to go to college.

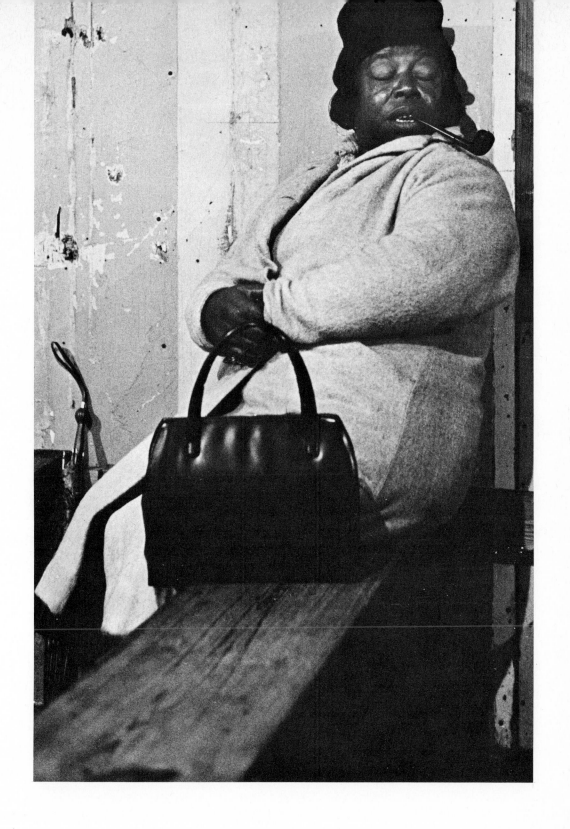

Mrs. Alice Wine
I DON'T HAVE ONE DAY HOME

That's what I'm doing now—working in a kitchen. I get up around five o'clock now, get on my clothes, wash my face and wash up, and I'll go to the back yard and feed chicken. From that I come back and clean up my house, and get out in the road and catch a ride and go to work. And I get to work I take off my coat, my hats, put on a apron and a hat, and go upstairs and get towels, and I wash those towels and put 'em on the line and come back in, start to clean rooms, make up beds. Then after I done do all that, then I come in the kitchen, get something to eat, and home I go. Well sometime I be waiting from three to four hours catching a ride.

I come back do a little work home, and leave from there to go on down to the Progressive Club and stay down there until about nine-thirty, ten o'clock, when it's a clear day. But when they having these party we don't leave 'til two and three in the morning. Get up next morning, go back on the job again. I don't have one day home.

On Sunday, go to church. I get up in the morningtime, get wash up and go outside feed my chicken and water 'em, and take my feet and go on down to the club and open 'em up. I be there around 'bout 'til eleven-thirty, catch a ride and go to church.

Come from church, I'll come back home and get dinner, and from there I go to the society meeting. Then the same Sunday evening we go to the hall to prayer meeting.

I don't have but a couple hours in everything I'm doing. But when I leave from home and come to someone house, like I here with you all now, I'm resting. And when I go home there's no rest. Something there for to do. Ain't nobody pushing me 'round; I'm pushing myself. I see it to do and I got it to do, so I just do it.

I don't care how hard I work in the day, if I get my night rest, it just like I ain't work that day. I get up that next morning, I don't feel it. But what put me down if I don't get my night rest. I get tired and don't feel like going. If I go to bed 'round seven-thirty, eight o'clock, I get up the next morning I don't feel nothing.

The Moving Star Hall congregation

I KNOW YOU'RE TIRED

I know you're tired_ now,_ sit down, I know you're tired now, _ sit down, I know you're tired_ now, sit down,

Sit down and rest a lit - tle while. You can tell it to your {ma - ma / sis - ter} while.

You can tell it to your {mama, / sister,} sit down,
You can tell it to your {mama, / sister,} sit down,
You can tell it to your {mama, / sister,} sit down,

Sit down and rest a little while.

You come from a distance, sit down . . . etc.

I know you weary, sit down . . . etc.

Oh sit down servant, sit down . . . etc.

I know you're tired now, sit down,
I know you're tired now, sit down,
I know you're tired now, sit down,
Sit down and rest a little while.

Mr. Joe Deas

I BEEN GOING IN THE CREEK
FOR FORTY-ODD YEARS

Fishing, yeah man, I been doing that for years. Get 'em with net; get 'em with line. Go down and push the boat overboard, go to bail 'em out, and go out casting. We go to Hut Creek, Willis Creek, then out to the sea. Great Lord, that's miles and miles out there—way out past the place they call Kiawah, then go out to the south. Get your whiting and trout. For mullet you go in the night. Course if you got a net, then you can go in the day and catch shrimp.

I make nets—knit 'em with cord and needle. Make my needle out of wood, board, tin. You can make 'em out of palmetto—take a branch of palmetto and cut 'em out of that. I make all most things myself—boat, net, two-wheel cart. If you ain't got that, you have to ride the ox

I do everything from the time I could turn around for myself. I been going in the creek for forty-odd years. Catched a ton of fish. Gone around and sell 'em to different people—make a living. I gone and got a license. Have to go to customs house and get license to go in the creek—get the fingerprint and all. When you come back from the creek, if you don't have enough to sell, you got enough for your family to eat.

That's the way we had to struggle in this world. But thank the Lord, we're here yet.

Mrs. Alice Wine
I CAN'T STAND TOO MUCH SITTING DOWN

If I be sitting down and don't have nothing to do, I get stove up. I get painful and lazy. I can't stand too much sitting down. I likes to go. You must be always active. You miss and sit around all day, lay around all night, you're so painful 'til you can't hardly get up. But you be working all the time, get your nerve together, get your vein together, then your muscle won't lock. Lot of people muscles lock by sitting down so much. No sit down for me. I likes to go.

I do any kind of job. I can plow, I can cut wood, I can sew, I can iron, I can scrub, I can do any kind of work in the field.

My husband was a farmer. He was a market man. He run a big farm. We have plenty chickens, plenty cow—two cow, and hogs. He get up and go to the market 'round two-thirty in the morning. Then I get up, put my baby to sleep, and get out there. Sometime we have these Columbia truck come in all time of night. These white people come in and carry these cabbage and thing. I'd be out there with them around four o'clock in the morning. After they go I come back to the house to see about the baby, then get in the tub and wash. Do all my washing, do my house cleaning, cook meals, have meals on time, cut cabbage, crate 'em too, pack 'em too.

I'm gone through a rough deal, but I thank God I'm still living. And I was doing those things in my nineteen and twenties. I'm fifty-nine now. So I'm not no baby!

Mr. Benjamin Bligen
I DO MY OWN WORK NOW

The first work I used to do was work on our own farm. I worked to help my father because they really had a hard time to raise us, and we just had to get out and do what we could to help in them days. We had to plant a garden.

Then my daddy was a fisherman, and I began to go in the river along with him and he teach me how to throw net, so I finally learn how to. And

he teach me how to paddle a boat. After he died, I took it up myself. I did the same thing: go in the river and catch some fish and sell it. Most of it is mullet fish, mullet and spots, and some catfish, all different kinds. Cast net. Run from three to four feet deep to maybe sometimes seven to eight feet deep. I go by myself or with my brother.

I began to do some carpenter work too. I was working along with a carpenter, and after a time I began to learn how to do some of the work for myself. So I finally try alone, and I made it all right. I do my own work now. I'm working at a block and pipe company—making door lintels and window lintels, all different kinds of stone.

The best kind of money people can make is on electricity works and 'chanical works and maybe expert carpenters and bricklayers. Harvesting season in the fall, you can't make much because it's only about three or four weeks long. You can do all right for those three or four weeks. You can make it anyhow. But 'round May and June, that's about the best months of the year on the farm. October you start having maybe some string beans. Then you sit 'til next year in May and June.

Mr. Benjamin Bligen
MORE LIGHT IS SHINING

I am forty. The look of the pudding is not the taste all the time. I have two children. I have a better time raising mine than my parents had raising us. Foods went up a lot, but still you can make it a little better now than you is in past time.

More light is shining. Can see more. Likewise you can do more and think more, 'cause I believe that more light is shining now than was shining in the past. And so help me God, I so glad that I can see some light. And I know there's more light for me. There is a bright light somewhere and I'm going to find it.

Mrs. Janie Hunter
I SEEM TO MAKE IT ALL RIGHT

When we first bought that piece of land in 1940, my husband was making thirteen dollars a week. I was washing and ironing for two person, and I wasn't making over three dollars a week. And we had to buy the land off that, and build that same house which burn down with that money, plus raise children. But I seem to make it all right. I get used to it. I get four dollars a day now, and it still don't seem much easier. Food cost more, clothes cost more, and the children takes more to go to school.

But the Lord didn't promise no human being to eat grass. Only horse and hogs eat grass. So he have a way paved for all those children, and we's had, if it be just one good meal a day. And I raise all of 'em up—hard time and good time—all is a healthy family. Didn't have no trouble 'til I lose my baby a year ago, and he wasn't sick but two days. But with the Lord, all things possible. And God give and He takes, and He takes nothing but His own. I know all those children belongs to the Lord, and He only give it to me for a special time. And I feel like He wants me to keep them children, He make a way for feed them. As the song say, "feed you when you hungry, and He clothes you when you naked." So up to this present minute I can say I have thirteen children living, and I thank God for all of them, and they is good children.

Mrs. Janie Hunter
THEY WANT ME TO TALK ABOUT THE PAST

I tell you, young people got a lot chance to think more in their age than I had to think in my days. 'Cause I couldn't think 'bout nothing but plant peas and corn in my days. But now these children got so much different thing to go through and learn, and they got nice schools. If they don't learn, it's nobody's fault but their own. Then I try to teach them these stories and different song and let them know what blues was like in my days coming up. My children like it. They sit down and they want me to talk about the past. They enjoy hearing it. I want them to know about it, so when I gone there be somebody to carry it on.

Mrs. Isabel Simmons
LIFE IS VERY DIFFERENT NOW

The old times was hard, but we still need religion right now. Life is very different now.

There is so much television here now; you didn't had that. It don't make life easier for me; it make 'em hard 'cause people stay home more. Lot don't go to church and different thing because they stay for see story. In them time only story you would hear tell, you tell your own story. This time, you watch television for story.

And the children now, they watch the TV and they take the thing on the TV to do just what they doing now. They think what is on the TV is real. But them time there doesn't be that kind of killing and shooting and cutting up like what going on now. Once in a while you hear about somebody die, but don't never hear about nobody get killed.

Mrs. Alice Wine
EVERYBODY SITTING ON THEIR OWN STOOPS

'Course that day, coming in 1919, all around like that, people was more friendly to one another. People come and sit with you and read the Bible. But these days you don't find anybody come visit. Everybody sitting on their own stoops. You don't find nobody to my house. When you're sick, people used to go around and have meeting for you and pray for you. Now the people who live in the house with the sick people got to come and ask somebody come pray for them. But before, people know you is sick. Not now. That's done pass.

Mrs. Mary Pinckney

IT'S TOUGH TO RAISE FIVE CHILDREN—SURE IS

I get married to the church. And I had the reception in Robbie Fields'
store. They had wine and piccolo playing, and dancing. I danced once. But
I couldn't dance 'cause my dress was too long. Long white dress, white shoes
and white veil 'cross my hair. Lot of people came to the church and lot of
people at the store. They had as much in the yard as was in the store,
couldn't come in. I guess 'round about three hundred head. Big wedding.

We was young children, growing up together. I met him long time ago,
but I didn't realize that was to be my husband today. I remember he was
picking the potato on the farm and I had to go work that morning and he

was there. I didn't have no partner to pick up potato with, so he say, "Come on; I'll be your partner." So we was partner for the day, picking up potato until over with. And when I get 'round about fifteen, sixteen years old, he come to my house and ask my mother can he keep my company. My mother ask me, will I accept it. First I say I don't know. So he come back and come back. And finally he wrote my mother a letter. Mother call me, she ask me, will I accept Arthur Lee company. So I say yes.

Those years keeping company I doesn't go out with no fellas, but I does see other boys, talk to them, go out to a party my brother be along. But I never love but one, and that's the one I get married to.

Now I'm twenty-five. I have five children. I work from seven in the morning 'til five-thirty in the evening—five days a week doing kitchen work. I mind five children, and when I get home I got to take care of five of my own.

My husband leave home 'bout six in the morning for he to wait on the road for a ride to go to work. He don't have he own transportation. He works out on contractor job, 'round about four years now.

It's tough to raise five children—sure is. My husband make 'round thirty, sometime forty dollars a week. And if it rain he don't bring in that because he don't work. I get paid for holiday when I'm off, but my husband don't get paid. He just have to wait it out. My mother used to take care of the children that aren't in school before the house burn down, but now I don't have anyone to take care of them. I have to stay off from work and start all over housewife again.

Miss Yvonne Hunter
ALL US WORKS

I am in third grade. I got left down one year because my mother was in New York one spring and I didn't have no shoes. I take arithmetic, language and reading. I like arithmetic best. When I grow up, if I don't be a secretary, I want to be a nurse.

For lunch at school we have popcorn, links, milk, roll, and have soup sometime. We have to pay for it. Sometime we take sandwich. At home we have grits, sometime rice for breakfast. Put milk and butter on rice. And have bread. Supper we have chicken and rice. Have greens, sometime cornbread and soup—vegetable soup. When Itchy and Joe go in the creek, we have oshters, crab, clams, fish.

Mother want us in bed at six o'clock. Sometime we go to bed seventhirty. Six sleep in a room. Tina and me sleep together, and Patricia and her two children sleep together, Mama and Papa sleep together, and Itchy sleep on the chair, and David and Johnny sleep on the couch.

We get up six o'clock. The bus come by at seven. School start at eightthirty. It takes five minute to get to school in the bus. I wash dishes before I go to school.

All us works. Sometime I wash dishes and I sweep the floor and I mop the floor. I cook. I cook grits, rice, cornbread. I cook meat, fry chicken, and I can make macaroni, and I can make salad.

I don't know if I want to get married. I don't like boys.

Mrs. Janie Hunter
IT'S A SMALL PLACE, BUT I RATHER
HAVE ALL MY FAMILY TOGETHER

I lost my house, a seven-room house, but I feel like it is the Lord's will. 'Cause I was burning oil stove from '41 up to now, and this have never happen to me before.

One day I went to work. I wash Tuesday night and leave a tubful of clothes for my daughter who always takes care of the house, and I told her to hang the clothes out. So she take my little battery radio in the yard under the tree, and she was hanging up the clothes, and when she look up, she saw smoke. She ran back to the house, but she couldn't even get in; the fire knock her back. She remember one of my little grand was sick in the house, and all she could do is run in the house and grab her. My son Johnny grab the rest of the children and take 'em over to my neighbor house and somebody call me.

One of my neighbor call me on my job, and my lady brought me home, must be about seventy mile an hour. I didn't feel so bad then, 'cause I thought fire engine would save at least some the furniture, but then I could see the housetop was falling in.

Then when everybody was together talking, I was sitting off by myself on Moving Star Hall, was thinking what would be best. I didn't feel like going anywhere far from the neighborhood. I have different friends offer me to come stay with them, and Mr. Jenkins, the place I raise on, he had a little empty house there, but I didn't want to go there either. I always want to be close to my meeting—Moving Star Hall.

So my neighbor, Nancy Field, she give me this little place she had built for the Florida people when they come. Those Florida people, they come 'round every year for season to pick tomatoes and thing, and she kept that little place for them. They just stays in it for a season—they'll stay any kind of where, you know.

It's a small place, but I rather have all my family together. If all of us have to sleep in one bed, I rather have all together. She kept manure and corn and all such of things in there, and all the rat been in there, but I was happy for it. I just get out and by my children, daughters, son, husband, they help me, and couple days we had it clean out, so now is clean enough to sleep in and eat in. We just work night and day. I sit up 'til two o'clock some nights. My son Johnny, he makes two window so it's light now. Then we go and buy a wood heater so it's very warm and comfortable.

We getting 'long all right. I realize God give and He takes. He take down and He can build back up. He took everything from Job—wife, children, Job have seven boys. His wife say Job ought to curse God and die. But Job say, "You speak as a foolish. When I curse my God and die, what will become of me? But I'll wait on my appointed time until my change will come." So I'll wait, 'cause I know soon or late there will be some change. If you only got faith in God, won't have nothing to worry about.

And everybody was so nice to me, and that one important thing make me feel good. All my friends from here and everywhere come and give; those who don't have to give, come with a word of encouragement. I appreciate everything they did. My brothers, my sisters, my daughters, friends, what they don't have to give, they come and sit and talk and sing together encouragement, and this make me understand that this is the Lord will.

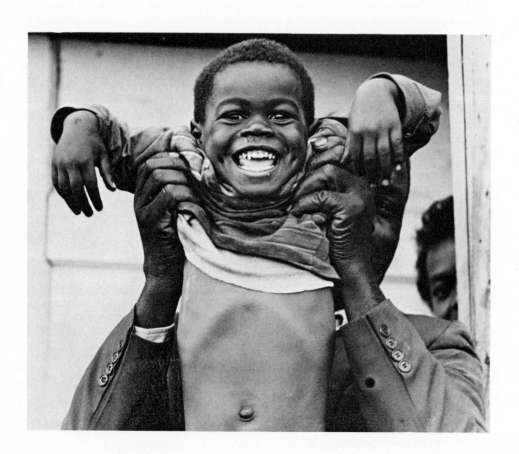

Mrs. Bertha Smith and
the Moving Star Hall congregation

THE STORM IS PASSING OVER

Sometimes I'm up, sometimes I'm down,
Sometimes I'm almost to the ground,
You know the storm is passing over,
Hallelu.

(CHORUS—2 TIMES)

Some say Peter, some say Paul,
Ain't but one God for we all,
You know the storm is passing over,
Hallelu.

The tallest tree in Paradise
Christians call the tree of life,
You know the storm is passing over,
Hallelu.

(CHORUS—2 TIMES)

3. ALL THINGS ARE

POSSIBLE IF YOU
ONLY BELIEVE

MEETING AT
MOVING STAR HALL

Mr. Esau Jenkins
SHOUTING FOR A BETTER DAY

Every Sunday night these people have meeting at Moving Star Hall. Every December 24th they have what we call a Christmas watch night meeting, and every December 31st, a New Year's watch. They sing from twelve o'clock until day clean.

They know the tune, they're ready to shout. They're giving praise to the great Supreme Being who have stood by them in the past days from slavery up to this present. Just to hear these songs remind us of our hardship. Those songs are the ones that made them happy, made them go through those hard days—the days when they didn't have a place to live of their own, didn't have a piece of land of their own, and were living on a plantation.

These people are hard-pressed people, and they are optimistic enough to believe that there are better days coming. When they get into these religious shouts, they feel so happy until that's all they can do but shout. The motions go into the hands and into the feet and they start clapping, and you can't keep them sitting—not when they start clapping, brother. They feel so happy 'til they got to shout. People sixty years and seventy years old clap and shout and jump all over the floor without falling down.

These people are trying to satisfy themselves, satisfy their soul. It's the only place they could be happy because life is so hard and sometimes there are any number of persons who do not know where the next meal is coming from. They can't talk back if they go on the farm regardless of how mean they were treated. Sometime their task they had was overburdening. Sometimes somebody watching them that they didn't have a chance even to stoop. They sometimes sad. But they're trying to get rid of it. If you could come and see them how they look when they singing and shouting, you can see they singing for a better day, shouting for a better day. And that's the thing that make them keep on shouting.

Mr. John Smalls
ANYTIME YOU COME, YOU IS IN

We don't charge nothing to come in Moving Star Hall. Moving Star Hall are free, and the door are open for each and every one. Whether you are white, whether you are dark like myself, or different color, come in. If you can preach, come on. We all preach. Don't say, no, you can't come up to this table. You can preach, pray, or testify. If you want speak, anything you want say, you got the opportunity—we give it to you.

'Cause we know we are in God hand. God made *all* of us. Don't make a few and somebody else made some; God made all. So I am happy to meet you all.

I hear the white madam say a while ago she glad we let 'em come in. "No, don't worry with that, Madam. Anytime you come, you is in. Bring friend, whatever; you's in." So sing, shout, get happy. But don't fall out!

Mrs. Janie Hunter

LEAD ME TO THE ROCK HIGHER AND HIGH*

* *Also sung elsewhere in the South "Lead Me to the Rock Higher Than I."*

(Chorus)

Won't you lead me to the rock higher and high,
Higher and high, higher and high,
Won't you lead me to the rock higher and high,
Shelter in the time of storm.

Oh King Jesus is a rock higher and high,
Higher and high, higher and high,
Oh King Jesus is a rock higher and high,
Shelter in the time of storm.

(Chorus)

Oh my God is a rock higher and high,
Higher and high, higher and high,
Oh my God is a rock higher and high,
Shelter in the time of storm.

Variant of verse:

Oh my God is a rock in a weary land,
Weary land, weary land,
God is a rock in a weary land,
Shelter in a time of storm.

86

Mr. James Mackey
SHOUT

That's so much the most thing I could do—shout. I'll tell you, with the spirit of God, you don't care what pain you got. You forget about that when you shout. When I going out, I feel so painful I scarcely don't go. But I say to myself, just as well if I go now, 'cause will come a day when the limbs fail me.

Mrs. Isabel Simmons
ALL JOIN AND MAKE THAT HALL

The only time they miss me at that hall, I either sick or off on some church duty. That hall mean a whole lot to me. It give me strength, spirit to carry on. I know everybody who comes. Some is friends, cousins, sisters; some neighbors.

I remember when Moving Star Hall was built, 'round about 1913, '14. Father help build the hall. Mother too. We all throw money until we gets enough to buy the land. All pay seven dollars for the lumber. All join and make that hall. They used to have prayer service in the house—only family then. Afterward, they began to have joint class from house to house. Then when we get the hall, we begin to have meeting there.

My daddy teach we how to sing, teach we how to shout, teach we how to go fast, teach we how to go slow. And then going to meeting, or later going to church, he'll teach we how to behave yourself when we get out to different place, before we leave home.

Used to be plenty people there—all them old people. They sing those old time spiritual, better than how we sing it now. Joe Bligen and Levy Green. Joe Deas was a good singer too, when he was much younger. Had plenty of singing womans, too.

That hall be full of people. Every Sunday. We have meeting in the neighborhood three time a week—Sunday and Tuesday and Thursday night. They keep a meeting going from eight until twelve. Then I get out, tomorrow morning I go on the farm make a day's work, too.

Mr. Joe Deas
THE SICK BENEFIT, AND DEATH BENEFIT

In the old days people couldn't afford insurance so we make up that Moving Star Society from ten cents each from Sunday School. We decided to bought a piece of ground to build that hall. And after we got 'em built we give 'em name: "Moving Star Hall." We got member from all different church. Generation after generation join and come out, join and come out. Some die and gone. The sick benefit. And death benefit. We still yet going on. By the help of the Lord we 'spect to go on 'til we are done.

Mrs. Alice Wine
THAT SOCIETY THERE, THEY TREAT YOU ALL RIGHT

Society is better than insurance to me. That society is supposed to tend the sick and bury the dead. Everybody who in there pay dues. They write from twenty-five cents up to one dollar a month. You is a twenty-five-cent member, you get twenty-five dollars when you die; you is a fifty-cent member, you get fifty dollars; you is a seventy-five-cent member, you get seventy-five dollars; you is a dollar member, you get a hundred dollars. Just as much as you pay, that's as much you get out. If you be sick, society service two person out to sit down with you all night, every night, until you get better or worse. If you don't go and sit, you be have to pay a dollar fine. If you sick and aren't able to pay your bills, they keep it up for you, live or dead; they elect money from the table and they keep you arrear. Insurance not going to do that.

And then the insurance man going to give you your money—put it on the table. Now, how you going to bury? That money can't move to dig grave. But that society there, they treat you all right. They don't give you your money and leave you there. They give you your money and give you attention. And we got pallbearers and everything in there. We got the pallbearers to take you from the undertaker and bring you to the church; take you from the church and carry you in the graveyard. They put you down there, and we got the member to cover you up. See, that's done.

Mr. John Smalls
EVERYBODY HAS A TURN

In the meeting, Brother Joe Deas, he are the oldest person in there, we takes him for the leading man. We put him in the front to take the text. Then take myself, I follow. Then whosoever I wanted to assist—Eli Smith or any other leader. And we go on that way. Everybody has a turn.

We have prayer service the first Sunday night in the month; and the second Sunday night let the brothers preach; then the third Sunday night we let the sisters testify; then we go right back on the fourth Sunday night the brothers will preach again. We used to had it just how it come. We feel like prayer meeting tonight, we have that. But later days, we decided we would mark it out, that every person would know where he going.

That way we trying to do it now. Brother Deas takes the text, when is preaching night, and the boys supposed to preach from that text he give you. You can go preach anywhere you want to preach, but you come right back to that same text.

Any individual, soon as the man finish preach, if you wanted to raise a song, you raise it. And another way, anytime we call someone up to preach, if anybody want to sing for you, can sing you up there. Then one can sing you down. Anybody. They can't sing long as you're talking; wait 'til you finish talk.

Mr. John Smalls
TURN THESE BIG FISH LOOSE

Now friends, we still moving on.
I'm not going to linger with you
'Cause I want to turn these big fish loose.

Brother Deas will come and set the foundation,
The road we going to travel by,
That all of you could know the way to go.

Mr. Joe Deas
TONIGHT YOU GOT A BLESSED CHANCE

I thank you for this great privilege I have before you.
You know from last January '64, I didn't have to been here.
My face could have been under the clay.
But at this same particular hour I have a chance
To rub shoulder to shoulder with you,
I can speak language to language,
I can look face to face.
It is a great joy.

Now we started on a new task, started a new race.
From the twenty-fifth morning we been running,
We been wrastling to behold this very hour of the night.
How many haven't lived to been able to see the day?
Some gone by car,
Some pass away with fire,
Some gone by water.

All part of the world is stirred up now.
Tonight you got a blessed chance to go to the house of God.
Some want to come out tonight and can't come,
And some can come that wouldn't come.
But the day will come.
The day will come.

Mrs. Janie Hunter
YOU HAVE A CHANCE TO EXPLAIN YOURSELF

You can feel yourself in that hall. You have a chance to explain yourself —anybody who want to. But in church on Sunday, we just have one preacher talk. And you might get a chance to raise a song or pick out one person to make a few remarks. But to that hall, everybody could have they way, tell your own story. That's the difference it makes.

Mr. John Smalls
GOOD MORNING WARRIORS

Good morning Warriors!
How y'all feel?
I'm feeling special alive.

I just rise to tell you all my aim
And whole heart's desire.
My desire is to go the whole way.
I give thanks for being brought
Not from just last December
But from an infant birth.

I can say, "Are we yet alive
To see each other's face."
Thank God for His redeeming grace.

Since last January
Rocky was my road,
Tedious was my journey.
What troubles have I seen,
What conflicts have I passed.

If I had ten thousand tongues
It wouldn't be enough
To give thanks to Thee
Who took my feet out of the miry clay
And put them on a solid rock.

Mrs. Mary Pinckney and the Moving Star Hall congregation
FIX ME JESUS

Fix me Je - sus, fix me right, Fix me so I can stand,

Fix my feet on a so - lid rock, Fix me so I can stand. (Oh, - - -)

Fix me Je - sus, fix me right, Fix me so I can stand, Oh,

Oh, fix me right, Fix me so I can stand.

fix my feet on a so - lid rock, Fix me so I can stand. Oh,

feet on a rock Fix me so I can stand.

My tongue tired and I can't speak plain,
Fix me so I can stand,
Fix my feet on a solid rock,
Fix me so I can stand.

Fix my home, Lord, fix it right . . . etc.

Fix my family, Lord, fix them right . . . etc.

Fix my neighbor, fix them right . . . etc.

Fix me warrior, fix me right . . . etc.

Fix me Jesus, fix me right,
Fix me so I can stand,
Fix my feet on a solid rock,
Fix me so I can stand.

Mr. Benjamin Bligen
A SERMON: LET NOT THEM THAT EAT DESPISE

I'm not gonna tarry before you, Warriors. I'm glad to be here to mingle my voice among my sisters and brothers. I hope and trust that if this sermon don't do you any good, I hope it won't do you no harm.

You know you can go from one part of the Bible to the other. God say we should love one another. Let not them that eat despise them that eat not. Let us remember one another. Don't let us be like Dives now. Let us try to be just as Lazarus. Dives despised the poor. Lazarus went and ask just for a crumb that fall from the table, and before Dives had the passion on him to give, he call the dog on him. But the poor beast have compassion and lick Lazarus.

Time going pass and go on. Time come along when the poor man die. He went on home to God and been at rest. Rich man Dives die, and his home was in Hell. When he lift up his eye in Hell and saw Lazarus in Heaven, he began to memorize. He know he didn't do right, but he cries, "Oh Father, let Lazarus come and dip his finger in the water and cool my trials and trouble."

God says, "No. You had all the good times, plenty of money. You didn't need Lazarus at that time. You need him now, but it too late."

Dives say, "I got five brother. Just give me a chance that I may go back and tell them to get their heart right, that they may shun this torment place I'm in."

And He say, "No. I got Moses and I got the prophets; let them hear what they say. If they don't believe the prophets, they won't believe you, Dives."

Pray for me, Warriors. Let us sing like we singing for the last time. Let us pray like we are praying for the last time. Take no thought for tomorrow, for tomorrow the sun may shine on your grave. Jesus told us to dig deep and lay your foundation on a solid rock, that when the storm of life blow against you, you're gonna find your Father rock. If you dwell upon Him, everythin' will be all right. The world can't do you no harm.

Mrs. Bertha Smith
I DON'T KNOW HOW FAR I'M GOING

Good morning, Warriors,
I'm sitting down right now,
I feel like singing and shouting, Jesus,
But I got to be very careful.
I don't know how far in '65 I'm going,
For my heart pump me from one side to the other,
And then it hurt me from one side to the other.
I don't know when my awful day will surely come
And then my appointed hour.

I can say this new brand morning
In another January,
"Are we yet alive to see each other's face."
Oh glory, and praise Jesus,
Give us of His dying and redeeming grace.
I know from last January,
Many days have I looked up on the highway
Wondering which way I must go.
Lord, you know I thank you for this hour of
The morning,
For I know it's none of my goodness,
I know if justice had plumb the line
All my daily travels would have cut off
And then never no more return.

If I shall cut off from God
I don't want to have no gathering to do.
I want to live so that I shall pass from
Life unto death.
I don't know if I going to be in my bed,
And then I don't know if I going to be on the highway.
I know this hour of the morning
I got peace with everybody,
And then I got peace
With all my neighbors' children.
I can say this hour of the morning,
I am just what I am.

Thank you, Jesus,
I don't know how far I'm going,
Got a pain racking the body right now.
And then I got to be very careful, Jesus.
I ask you all to pray for me
So I may be able to run on.

Mrs. Janie Hunter and the Moving Star Hall congregation
ASK THE WATCHMAN HOW LONG

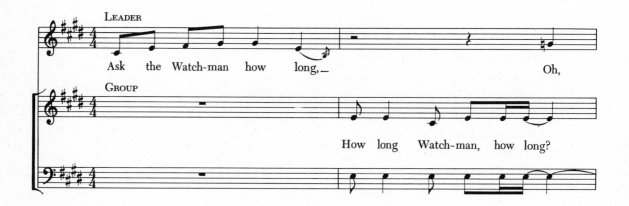

LEADER: Oh ask my brother how long,
GROUP: How long Watchman, how long?

In sixty-four how long? . . . etc.
Well, ask my daughter how long . . . etc.
Well, ask my preacher how long . . . etc.

Oh all my neighbors, how long? . . . etc.

Oh before the roll call . . . etc.
Oh just a few more risings . . . etc.
Oh ask my leader how long . . . etc.

We don't know___ how long,___ Oh,___

Oh,___ how long Watch-man, how long?

Well, all my neighbors how long? . . . etc.

Oh soon it will be over . . . etc.
Watchman, how long? . . . etc.
You know how long, how long . . . etc.
Ask my friends how long . . . etc.

Brother Jenkins, how long? . . . etc.

Oh, how long, how long,
How long Watchman, how long?
How long, how long,
How long Watchman, how long?

Mr. Benjamin Bligen and the Moving Star Hall congregation
REBORN AGAIN

LEADER: Won't you reborn Member, won't you reborn again,
GROUP: Oh, reborn again.
LEADER: Well, you must keep a-rollin', got to reborn again,
GROUP: Oh, reborn again.

Oh, reborn warriors, won't you reborn again,
Oh, reborn again.
Yes, you can't get to Heaven 'less you reborn again,
Oh, reborn again.

Oh, goin' to the river, gonna take my walk,
Oh, reborn again.
Meet Jesus mother, gonna stand and talk,
Oh, reborn again.

Just let me put on my travelin' shoes,
Oh, reborn again.
I'm goin' to Heaven, gonna carry the news,
Oh, reborn again.

Let me tell you the natural fact,
Oh, reborn again.
Can't get to Heaven, ain't comin' back,
Oh, reborn again.

When I get to Heaven, gonna sing and shout,
Oh, reborn again.
There ain't nobody there gonna turn me out,
Oh, reborn again.

When I get to Heaven, gonna sit right down,
Oh, reborn again.
Ask Jesus mother for my starry crown,
Oh, reborn again.

Oh Satan is mad and I'm so glad,
Oh, reborn again.
Lost the soul he thought he had,
Oh, reborn again.

Oh Satan he walking like a snake in the grass,
Oh, reborn again.
He always walk in a Christian path,
Oh, reborn again.

Wonder what Satan keep growlin' about,
Oh, reborn again.
He chained up in Hell and he can't get out,
Oh, reborn again.

Oh one of these mornings and it won't be long,
Oh, reborn again.
I'll see some grapes a-hanging down,
Oh, reborn again.

I pick a grape and I suck the juice,
Oh, reborn again.
Sweetest grape I ever taste,
Oh, reborn again.

Reborn, reborn, reborn again,
Oh, reborn again.
Can't get to Heaven 'less you reborn again,
Oh, reborn again.

Rev. James Grant
GET ON YOUR HOLY HORSE

Be careful, my friends, because sometimes the
Chairman of Hell begin to saddle up his pony.
He gonna override somebody.
You walk down the road
And somehow your feet begin to be tangled.
The road become rocky, hard to cross.

Hallelujah, my friends,
Put on your travelin' shoes.
Get on your holy horse
Because sin are now pressing hard,
Many dangers follow.

Mr. Benjamin Bligen

I REALIZE I'M HERE FOR SOME PURPOSE

I was about twenty-seven when I start to go to Moving Star Hall regular. Since I was a little boy, Mom used to take me there on her back—I was so small to walk in the dark, you know.

There was a time when blues was all that was on my mind. But the truth is the light, and after getting old in age I realize that I'm here for some purpose. Father always teach me the Bible, teach us how to sing and how to pray, and tell us what must not do and what must do to inherit life everlasting. So I stop and ask myself some question. Then I just had to change from singing blues and begin to go back to what my old parents said—singing spiritual songs.

And I found out that's better.

Mr. William Saunders

THIS IS GOOD, BUT IT DOESN'T HELP YOUR EATING

We all as kids went to Moving Star Hall. As far as I was concerned, I just had to be there. We used to enjoy the singing and the shouting. And at a certain period of the night, all the youngsters in there had to go up front and kneel down and everybody prayed. That place used to be full—three nights a week. You couldn't get in that place if you be late on Sunday nights. And it was so much young people. All of a sudden it just start dying off.

For one thing most of the young people started going away. Like me, I went in the Army. I was about fifteen. Once the kids start going to different places, and we start to be more enlightened, then we start getting away from this old type of thing. As we get more education, we come to find out that this wasn't the type of thing we needed to help us through the world. We needed more than this. This is good, but it doesn't help your eating. Why waste time with something that you aren't gonna get anything out of at all? You gonna be looking forward to when you die, and man, you hungry now.

That Moving Star Hall business just about died out completely. Then they started building it back up again. Now some of the people, the Moving Star Hall Singers, are enjoying some of the fruit of their labor.

Mr. James Mackey
MORNING

Here am I again once more, Heavenly Father,
The worm of the dust
Ready to bow this hour of the morning
On my bruised and bending knee.
Thank you, My Father, for your guardin' angel,
That guard me all night long
Until morning light appear.
And before he went from his watch,
He touch my eyes this morning with a finger of love,
And my eye become open
And behold a brand new Monday morning.
Oh, God, if you so please
Give us that holding out spirit,
That you may own us all
When we done trod across the many street of Charleston.
Oh God, what I say for our neighbors,
And the neighbors' children around in this vicinity,
Oh please, Our Father,
Make them more patient, more acknowledge,
May we love each and one another.
Help us to help each other.
And each other's cross to bear.
And Our Father, if you please,
Remember the President of this United States,
Oh, remember the officials.
And Our Father, once more I say
For the President of the N.A.A.C.P.,
Throw thy arms of protection around them,
May they achieve victory in whatever they may undertake to do.
Lead them, Our Father,
Through the unfriendly world where there's no friendly grace.
We know we must fight to increase our courage
That we may be able to endure the pain.
I ask you to please remember mankind far away,
Whatever his town may be.
Make him realize, that awful day will surely come.
And then have mercy, My Father,
When I done walk the last mile of the way,
Done all that you 'signed my hand to do,
When I shall come down off the stage of action,
Must surrender under the black banner of Death,
Ask you, Jesus, give me a resting place
Somewhere in your Kingdom
Which Job declare
The wicked cease from troubling.
Amen.

Mrs. Ruth Bligen

ALL THINGS ARE POSSIBLE IF YOU ONLY BELIEVE

On - ly be - lieve,_____(Well, you) on - ly be - lieve,____ (You know that)

'all things are pos - si - ble, If you on - ly be - lieve. (Just trust Him now__)

ALTERNATE VERSION

On - ly be - lieve, _ (Well,_ you) on - ly be - lieve,_____

All things are pos - si - ble, If you on - ly be - lieve.
(Keep on prayer-in' if you)

°a) variant

lieve, (nev - er doubt Him now) __

Only believe, (well, you) only believe,
(You know that) all things are possible,
If you only believe.

(Just trust Him now) only believe, (well, you) only believe,
All things are possible,
If you only believe.

(Keep on prayerin', if you) only believe, only believe,
All things are possible,
If you only believe.

(Tell the warriors, if you) only believe, only believe,
All things are possible,
If you only believe.

Only believe (never doubt Him now), only believe,
(You know that) all things are possible,
If you only believe.

(He'll be your {mother, if you) only believe, only believe,
{father,
All things are possible,
If you only believe.

4. TALKIN' 'BOUT

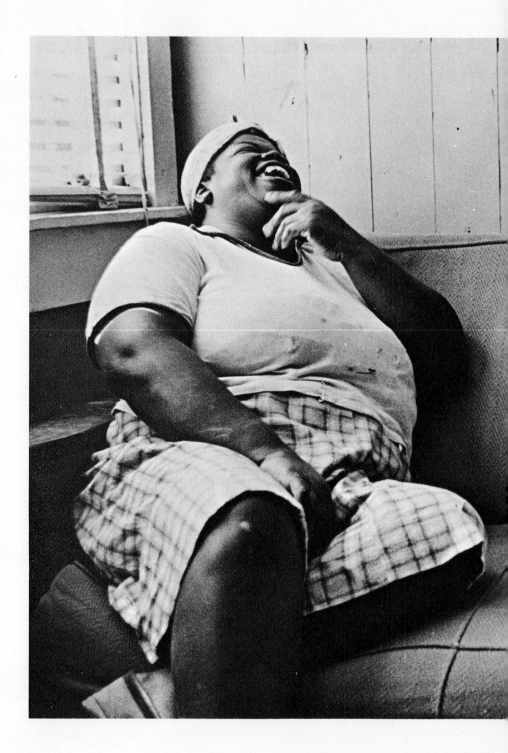

JOKEY

A GOOD TIME

TIMES

Mrs. Janie Hunter
STORIES

When we was small, we didn't 'low to go no place, but we have all we fun at home. On weekend when we do all work what told to us and after we finish work at night, we sit down and we all sing different old song, and parents teach us different game and riddles. We go and cut the wood and wrap up the house with green oak and muckle wood, then we all stays by the fire chimbley and listen to stories.

JACK AND MARY AND THE DEVIL

This is a old story. Very old. Way back in the time I heard my old parents talk about. Slavery time. Time when the Yankee beat the Rebel. They said it was a true-life story of Jack and Mary.

Jack and Mary was brother and sister. Mary was old enough to keep company, so a young man come to Mary mother house one day, and ask Mary mother could he keep Mary company. Mother ask Mary, "Do you love him?" And she said yes. So mother tell him, "Yes, I don't mind."

So after a while Mary mother tell this young man that he could take her out. But Mary didn't know who this young man was; this young man was the Devil. He had horse feet and he had horn on his head, but he had all of 'em cover.

Jack heard his mother tell Mary she could go, so he went and say, "Mama, could I go with my sister?"

She say, "I don't mind if Mary don't mind." But Mary tell Jack, "No, I don't want you to go with me; you is too young."

The old Devil had a high-top buggy and horse. And Jack had a horse. Well Jack was a very wise boy, so he study a plan, and full his pocket with corn. Then Jack went on ahead, and he get in a store and turn into a gold ring. All that time Mary and her boyfriend get in the cart and began traveling. When they get to the store Mary said, "Oh, I love that ring."

The old Devil—young boyfriend—say, "Jump out and price it."

The man say, "Nine thousand dollar."

Devil say, "Well that just my pocket change." So he got it. All that time Mary didn't know she brother turn to a ring in the store, and that's the very ring Mary have love. She put her brother on her finger and didn't know. And all that time they travel until they get to this young man home. And when they go in, oh he had a beautiful home.

Then when time come to eat she ask what they are going have for supper. He say, "Oh, pull out one of them drawer and cook one them dead man in there."

And then Mary began to get trouble in mind. She realize she was down in Hell. She said, "Lord, when my brother have want to come with me, I should of saw right and let him come."

And then, Jack disappear off Mary finger, say, "Oh Sister, when I ask to come with you, you run me back, but how now?" And then Mary was so happy. Then when time come for go to bed that old Devil put her to bed and fall on the floor and start for sleep. Mary knew that Jack was on her finger. As soon as the old boy got fast asleep, Mary and Jack began to travel.

Well the old Devil had a rooster; he was a teller. And as they began to travel, old Rooster get in the Devil face and spur 'em. Say:

Maus - sa, _____ your Miss is _____ gone _____ I hear - in' the bell say 'bal a long.' _____

Devil say, "How long gone?"
Say, "Long time."
Then he tell the rooster, "Go down yonder and get my old bull that jump fifty mile away." And the Devil get on the old bull back, say:

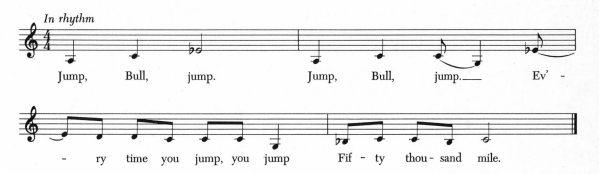

Jump, Bull, jump. Jump, Bull, jump. _____ Ev' - - ry time you jump, you jump Fif - ty thou - sand mile.

Well, he made one jump, he jump right by Jack and Mary, and Jack drop one grain corn, and it turn a ocean of water. And all that time it take for that water to dry up, Jack and sister was far away. Then the Devil made a loud cry, saying:

Ma - ry, _____ How you get o - ver here? _____

Mary say:

I drink,__ My horse drink,__ My broth-er drink,__

'Til I____ Get o - ver here.____

Old Bull say:

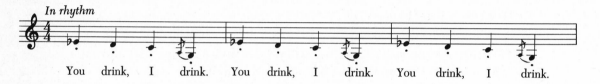

You drink, I drink. You drink, I drink. You drink, I drink.

He drink, and bust the bull belly loose, and when he think the bull was going fifty thousand mile an hour, the bull couldn't make but five mile an hour. And old Devil take some string and tie the old bull belly up. And all that time Jack and Mary was far away. Then he get on the old bull back and say:

You jump, I jump. You jump, I jump. You jump, I jump.

Ev' - ry time you jump, you jump Fif - ty thou - sand mile.__

And jump right by Mary and Jack. Then Jack drop another grain of corn, and it turn a whole mountain, 'cross and 'cross the world. Old Devil say:

"Mary,
How you get
Over here?"

118

Mary say:

> "I climb,
> My brother climb,
> My horse climb,
> 'Till I get
> Over here."

Bull say:

> "You climb, I climb,
> You climb, I climb,
> Every time you climb,
> You slide back down."

Now he couldn't climb. Every time the bull climb to catch Mary and Jack, he slide back down. And when he did climb the old mountain down, then Jack and Mary was across a bridge another three miles away, and he was about getting given up in mind. He say:

> "Mary, tell me how you
> Get over here?"

Mary say:

> "I root, my brother root,
> My horse root,
> 'Till I get over here."

Bull say:

> "You root, I root,
> You root, I root,
> You root, I root."

Then old Devil and old Bull root beneath the pine tree, and that pine tree fall 'cross the bridge, the bridge bend, and that's the way that story end.

Mr. Benjamin Bligen

THE RABBIT AND THE WOLF AT THE DANCE

The Rabbit and the Wolf been going to a dance one night, and the Rabbit tricky, you know. The Rabbit was in love with the Wolf girlfriend, and the Rabbit want to get close to she. So after they went to a joint, and the music start to play, Rabbit ask Wolf girlfriend to dance. It was a fast dancing record, but Rabbit walk up and tell Wolf, "Wolf, this music call for close dance." He tell Wolf that music call for close dance that he would get a chance to talk with the Wolf girlfriend. Well, the Wolf see him dancing close with the girlfriend, Wolf wouldn't take it for no harm. That was cut and dry, see. Cut and dry.

Mrs. Janie Hunter

THE RABBIT AND THE PARTRIDGE

Everybody think that a rabbit have the most sense, but one day the Partridge outsensed the Rabbit. This day the Partridge went out on a walk, come back home with his head under his wing. On the way back he stopped at Bunny Rabbit's house and say, "Oh Rabbit, how you like my head?" And all the time he had he head under he wing.

Rabbit say, "I like it fine; where *is* your head?"

Partridge say, "You old fool Rabbit, you ain't got no sense. I leave my head home for my wife shave."

The Rabbit take off and went home to his wife, say, "Old Gal, I got a job for you. Come on and chop my head off. I want you to give me a haircut."

She say, "Oh Rabbit, no! I not supposed to cut your head off. If I cut your head off you'll die."

Rabbit say, "No I won't die either, 'cause the Partridge cut he head off, leave 'em home for he wife to shave. I don't see why I can't cut mine off."

So he argue and argue until he make his wife get the knife, and the wife chop the old Bunny head off. And then the Bunny die. The old lady cry. Then she skin the rabbit and eat him.

The old lady went to the Partridge and say, "Partridge, why you did that?" Say, "Why you take your head under your wing and fool the Bunny that you leave your head home for your wife to shave, when you know it wasn't true?"

Partridge say, "Well, you ain't no fool, and if you'll only keep that up, we sure will get along." After that the Partridge have two wives—have his wife and then the Bunny's wife.

BARNEY McCABE

We learn some these stories from my uncle, Harry Williams. He was kind of rough, but he really could tell some stories.

Once upon a time it was a twin sister and brother. The sister name was Mary and the brother name was Jack. One day they decided to go on a long traveling. But Jack was a wise child and he told Mary to go in the house and ask Mother could we go. Her mother say, "Yes, you could go, but take care." So Jack say, "Wait a minute, Sister," and went to the barn and get four grain of corn. And Mary said to Jack, "What you gonna do with that corn?" Jack said, "In a long while, you will see." So he put the corn in his pocket.

Then before he leave home Jack told his mother, say, "Mama, I got three dogs—Barney McCabe, Doodle-le-doo and Soo-Boy. I going to leave a glass of milk on the table. If you see that glass of milk turn to blood, I want you to turn my dogs loose."

So they went on traveling and all the time wondering what was the end going be. Pretty soon it come dark and they begin to get weary. They knocked at an old lady house. The old lady run to the door, say, "Who is it?"

Jack say, "Me, Mama. Could we spend the night here? 'Cause we far from home and we very tired." Old lady say, "Oh yes, come on in."

All that time she was a witch-craft and the children didn't know it. She fed them and put them to bed. She had a knife she call "Tommy Hawk." After she put the children to bed she began to sharpen it up:

Penny, get your knife, Penny, get your knife, Penny, get your knife, go shock 'em, shock 'em. Hump back a Josie back a see Antony, Mama and your daddy tell me so, See so, I think it so Tam-a-ram-a-ram.

Children say, "Grandma, what's all that noise? We can't sleep."

She say, "That ain't nothing but your grandma frock-tail switchin' to get your supper hot. You all go back to sleep."

So Jack begin to wonder how they can get out of there. Then he remember the old lady have a room full of pumpkin. Jack takes two pumpkin and put 'em in the bed and cover 'em over, pretend it was he and his sister. Then Jack throw one grain of corn to the window, and it turn into a ladder. Jack and Mary climbed the ladder down and they start traveling for home.

The old lady sharpen her knife faster:

"Penny, get your knife,
Penny, get your knife,
Penny, get your knife, go shock 'em, shock 'em.

Hump back a Josie back a see Antony,
Mama and your daddy tell me so,
See so, I think it so
Tam-a-ram-a-ram."

She didn't hear no noise, so she sneak in the room and chop up the pumpkins in the bed. Then she ran in the kitchen and got a dishpan, and pull back the cover. And when she think she putting the meat in the pan for cook for breakfast, she drop the pumpkin in the pan. And Jack and Mary was long gone.

She get mad, grab Tommy Hawk and flew down on those children. The children drop another grain of corn and it turn a tall pine tree. And Jack and Mary flew up in that tree. The old lady start cut on the tree, say:

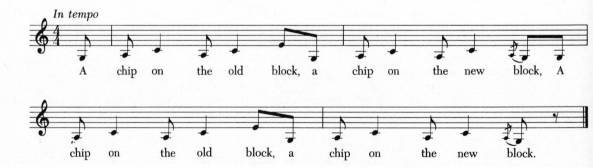

Then Jack drop a grain of corn down from the pine tree, and back home that glass of milk turn to blood. Them dogs begin to holler. Jack's mother ran in the yard and turned the dogs loose. Jack say:

Freely

Bar - ney Mc - Cabe, and Doo - dle - le - doo, _____ and Soo -
Boy, _____ Your maus - sa call - ing you.

Dogs say:

In tempo

Maus - sa, Maus - sa, com - ing all the time, _____
Maus - sa, Maus - sa, com - ing all the time. _____

Old witch say:

> "A chip on the old block, a chip on the new block,
> A chip on the old block, a chip on the new block."

Every time she chip, the tree lean and lean. Jack call:

> "Barney McCabe, and Doodle-le-doo, and Soo-Boy,
> Your maussa almost gone."

Dogs say:

> "Maussa, Maussa, coming all the time,
> Maussa, Maussa, coming all the time."

Jack drop another corn, the last corn, and it turn a bridge. And then when the old witch pull the ax up for take the last chop and chop Jack and Mary in the head, the dogs ran up. Barney McCabe cut her throat, Doodle-le-doo suck her blood and Soo-Boy drag her on the bridge, the bridge bend and that's the way that story end.

Mrs. Mary Pinckney
I TOO SCARED THEN

People say if you look over your left shoulder you'll see ghosts. Tell about hag and all kind of thing like that. I look back over my left shoulder all the time, I don't see no ghost. I never see none, but I believe in ghost. Some call 'em ghost, some call 'em spooks, boodyman. That's the way we is call 'em when we was little—boodyman.

That old man, Michael Brown, he's always be to our house. I guess he's 'round about seventy-five. He is come over every Sunday and he sit down and talk about all these old-time thing. Talk about old-time ghost. He say when he go home nighttime he have to carry a stick and feel his way, 'specially if it dark, 'cause ghost is crowded in the path. He take stick go "whicha-whoocha-whoocha," clear his way. I be glad when he go home 'cause he talk about those thing and make me scared. Mama like to listen. Not me. I say, "Take your hat and go home." I too scared then. Ghost!

Mr. James Mackey
THEY'LL KNOCK YOU OFF YOUR FOOT

Some people died, their spirit walk around. If a person died happy, they don't bother you. But people died bad, well, they'll knock you off your foot.

One most knock me off my foot one night. I was coming out just about dusk-dark and something come around me like a long black snake—tie around me. It shoot up and I ain't feel like I was onto the ground at all. Only way I came back in this world, a dog smell my scent and that dog bark. Didn't for that, I'd been *gone*.

When my foot touch ground, feel like I been off the ground. I go and curse 'em. They say if I pray I might of get off much better. The more I curse, the more I guess he try to knock me.

When the feeling get back to me, then I start to walk—taking my time just like when a person sick—and I could imagine he up behind me. My hair on my head just tauten up. I got back home, gone to bed that night with *all* my clothes on.

Mrs. Janie Hunter

WHEN YOU GET TO OLD AGE YOU TURN A HAG

I say see it to believe it. Ghosts shows up to some people, and some people they don't. But I'm not scared of 'em. I'm more scared of live.

But hags, that's real. When you get to old age, you turn a hag. Hags come to your house and hag your children. Children can't sleep, or a hag take somebody child and put 'em under the bed. Sometime a hag sit on you and keep you from getting up, try to smother you.

But you could tell a hag. I heard my old people say, if you want to tell a hag, put a broom 'cross your door. If that's a hag, he going take up that broom, ain't going step across it.

If hag bother you, use salt and pepper. Sprinkle either by your bed or 'cross your door and they won't come in. The salt burn their skin.

Mrs. Mary Pinckney

I GOT A BLUESY FEELING

I like blues. My uncles Benji and Willis—oh, they could sing! Willis is come home 'round twelve and one o'clock in the night and wake up everybody on the hill. Go one side by the pump and he sing that blues from then 'til four in the morning. Wake up everybody. Mama is come outside, say, "Willis, why don't you come on in the house?"

"Can't come in the house right now, Doll, I got a bluesy feeling." He sing.

And Benji, Benji could sing! He have one them cowhorn and he get up and put it to his mouth and blow 'em. Just like a trumpet. And Willis be singing the song and he be blowing the horn and they going down the road blowing and singing. And I be right there listening to 'em. I follow them too. They is like for I follow them 'cause I sing right along with them.

My brothers sing blues too. Joe, he like all different kind of song—spiritual and blues. Sometime he be home by heself and go on the road or stay on that porch or go under a tree, sit down and just play his guitar and sing his song. And I'll go and help him.

Mr. Joe Hunter

WHAT YOU GONNA DO?

What you gon - na do when Ja - nie leave you, Wil - lie, what you gon - na do? What you gon - na do when Ja - nie leave you, Wil - lie, what you gon - na do?_____ She said, "Bye, bye, Wil - lie, I don't want you no more,__ Pack up all my clothes I'm gon - na leave this town,"____ What you gon - na do when Ja - nie leave you, Wil - lie, what you gon - na do?

What you gonna do when Janie leave you, Willie, what you gonna do?
She said, "Bye bye, baby, I don't want you no more",
Sitting here crying, Janie, please don't go,
What you gonna do when Janie leave you, Willie, what you gonna do?

What you gonna do when Janie leave you, Willie, what you gonna do?
She said, "Bye bye, Willie, I'm putting you down,
Pack up my clothes I'm gonna leave this town",
What you gonna do when Janie leave you, Willie, what you gonna do?

Mrs. Janie Hunter
WATER MY FLOWERS

Oh, wat - er my flow - ers, bloom - ing in the air so high, We are young

la - dies and we will sure - ly die. All sad is Y - vonne, she is a nice young

la - dy. Why not she, why not she, Turn her back and call her sweet - heart

name? Mis - ter Jun - ey, Mis - ter Jun - ey is a nice young man, He come to the door with he

hat in he hand. He ask for Miss Y - vonne, Up - stairs, down - stairs, sew - ing on a ma - chine.

Pull off your glove and show your ring,__ To - mor - row, to - mor - row is Thanks - giv - ing.

Doc - tor, Doc - tor, Can't you tell?__ What is the mat - ter with Y - vonne now?__

She is sick__ and she go - ing to die.__ That__ gon - na make - a Mis - ter Jun - ey cry.__

The Hunter and Pinckney children

SALLY ROUND THE SUNSHINE

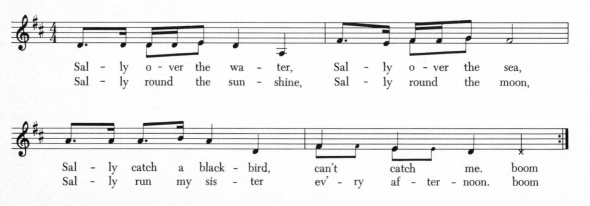

Sal — ly o — ver the wa — ter, Sal — ly o — ver the sea,
Sal — ly round the sun — shine, Sal — ly round the moon,

Sal — ly catch a black — bird, can't catch me. boom
Sal — ly run my sis — ter ev' — ry af — ter — noon. boom

130

Mrs. Janie Hunter, Mrs. Mary Pinckney, and their children

OLD LADY COME FROM BOOSTER

Old la-dy come from Boos-ter, She had two hen and a roos-ter, The roos-ter died, the old la-dy cried, She could-n't get egg like she use-ter. Oh, Ma, you look so, Oh, Pa, you look so. Who been here since I were gone?___

Two lit-tle boy with the blue cap on.___ Hang 'em on a___ hick-'ry stick, Rank-y tank-y___ down my shoe, The Buf-fa-lo Boy gon-na buy it back. Pain-y me hip, Rank-y tank-y. Pain-y me knee, Rank-y tank-y. Pain-y me leg, Rank-y tank-y. Pain-y me el-bow, Rank-y tank-y. Pain-y me shoul-der, Rank-y tank-y. Pain-y me neck, Rank-y tank-y. On___ up to me head,___ Rank-y tank-y. Don't___ leave me here, Rank-y tank-y.___ Old la-dy come from Boos-ter, She had two hen and a roos-ter. The roos-ter died, the old la-dy cried, She could-n't tell the news like she use-ter.

131

Mrs. Janie Hunter, Mrs. Mary Pinckney,
and their children

SHOO TURKEY SHOO

SOLO

An - nie?   You see my tur - key?   Which

GROUP

Ma'am?_____   Yes,   ma'am._

side   he   go - in'?   Will   you   help   me   catch   him?

So   and   so   and,

Get   read - y   let's   go. _   Shoo   tur - key,   shoo,   shoo,

Yes,   ma'am.   Shoo   tur - key,   shoo,   shoo,

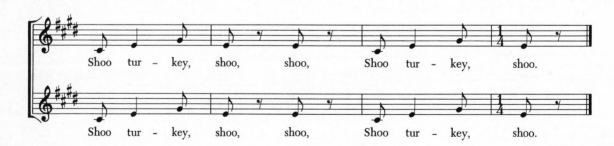

Shoo   tur - key,   shoo,   shoo,   Shoo   tur - key,   shoo.

Shoo   tur - key,   shoo,   shoo,   Shoo   tur - key,   shoo.

Clapping pattern often used

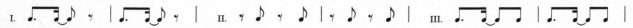

132

SOLO: Annie?
    GROUP: Ma'am?
SOLO: You been to the wedding?
    GROUP: Yes, ma'am.
SOLO: Did you get any cake?
    GROUP: Yes, ma'am.
SOLO: How nice that taste?
    GROUP: Nice, nice.

Annie?
    Ma'am?
Did you been to the wedding?
    Yes, ma'am.
Did you get any wine?
    Yes, ma'am.
How nice that taste?
    Nice, nice.

Annie?
    Ma'am?
You see my turkey?
    Yes, ma'am.
Which side he gone?
    So, so.
Will you help me catch him?
    Yes, ma'am.
Get ready, let's go.
ALL: Shoo turkey, shoo, shoo,
    Shoo turkey, shoo, shoo,
    Shoo turkey, shoo, shoo,
    Shoo turkey, shoo.

Miss Yvonne Hunter
A LOT OF KIDS PLAY THOSE GAMES

I learn some songs and games from my mother, some from my brother, and then I learn some in school. A lot of kids play those games. Mostly girls. Kids that are seven, eight, nine, ten, eleven, twelve play. There are some that don't like to play the games.

It's no music teacher at school. Our teacher have times for teaching songs. They have piano. When Mama teach us songs, she teach us until we learn it good.

Mr. Benjamin Bligen and the Moving Star Hall congregation
TALKIN' 'BOUT A GOOD TIME

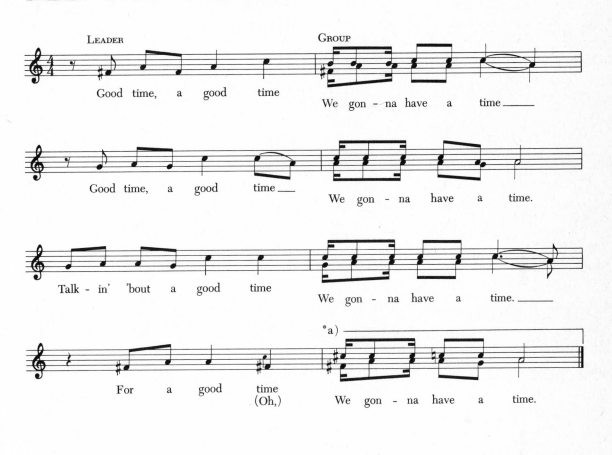

LEADER

Good time, a good time

GROUP

We gon - na have a time ____

Good time, a good time ____

We gon - na have a time.

Talk - in' 'bout a good time

We gon - na have a time. ____

°a)

For a good time
(Oh,)

We gon - na have a time.

°a) variant

We gon - na have a time.

LEADER: Singing for a good time,
GROUP: We gonna have a time,
LEADER: For a good time,
GROUP: We gonna have a time.

Praying for a good time . . . etc.

Let's have a good time . . . etc.

Talkin' 'bout a good time,
We gonna have a time,
For a good time,
We gonna have a time.

5. DOWN ON ME

RACE RELATIONS

Mr. Joe Deas

YOU IS ABEL CHILDREN AND I'M A CAIN

There ain't but two race. Two brother children. If you don't work with me I ain't work with you. You can't do without me and I can't do without you. You may don't want me to your table, but you can't do without me. Cain and Abel—you is Abel children and I'm a Cain. So I got to work with you and you got to work with me. Ain't but two race, and there ain't but two place to go—that's Hell and Heaven. If you miss that, you just forever done. That's all.

Miss Laura Rivers
THAT'S ALL RIGHT

CHORUS

That's all right,_____ that's all right _____ That's all__ right,_____

that's all right._ Since my soul__ got a seat up in the King - dom,_

VERSE

That's all right._ Hush lit - le__ ba - by,__ don't you cry,__ You

know your_ moth-er been_ born to die.__ Since my soul__ got a

seat up in the King dom,_____ That's all right.__

°a) variant

That's all right _____

You go brute me, you go scorn me,
You go scandalize my name.
Since my soul go a seat up in the Kingdom,
That's all right.

(CHORUS)

One of these mornings, it won't be long,
You ask for me and I'll be gone.
Since my soul . . . etc.

Two white horses side by side,
One of those horses Jesus ride.
Since my soul . . . etc.

(CHORUS)

Mrs. Betsy Pinckney
YOU CAN BE BLACK OR SCARLET

Now some people after slavery times think to themselves, "If I see a white and he needs help, but they didn't tell me to do it, I wouldn't do it anymore." But me, I go there and they ain't call me neither. He need help and his family need it, and that's the reason God help some people to get along so good.

I treat everybody right; my heart open for all. And that's why people treat me well for it. That's right! Sometime I pick the bean and I say, "I ought to give 'em a quart of bean." Well, when I send that bean, how they glad.

I don't care what kind of people, I going there and help 'em. I do it, sir. I got proof! You can be black or scarlet but it don't make no difference. The pure in heart shall see God.

Mrs. Alice Wine
NOW THE WORLD IS NOTHING BUT WHITE PEOPLE

When I were growing up, I must have seen one white man in my life. And I was so scared of that white man I never see his face. You might see but two white man in the whole Johns Island then. But now the island is full of white people. There so many white people it seem like there always one now. Before then you wouldn't see no white people there in six or seven months. But now, the world is nothing but white people. White people!

The Bible says you must love your fellow mans, 'gardless of what color you are, you must love 'em. Ain't no need for I love my color, hate you. 'Cause God don't please with it. 'Cause we all is God's children. We must love one another.

The church doesn't do a thing for you no more than preach a sermon. That's all the preacher do for you. But you got to live a life living right here. The way you walk and the way you talk, the way your action—there's your sermon right there. You preaching your sermon before you die.

The way you treat people, that's your heaven right there. Now if you born dumb, you just dumb. If you're a mean person all your life, you're just a mean person; people can't say good for you. If you're a good person all your life, that's all people will say is he's a good person. Got to first have heaven here before you have Heaven. If you have speck in your heart, you cannot get in God's kingdom. I never been up there yet, but I feel about it.

Mr. William Saunders
I COULD HAVE BEEN SOMEBODY

I apply for a job and you apply for a job, and I'm the better man, then I should get the job, not you because you're white. I believe to myself that the biggest mistake that I've made was not being born white. To me I could have been somebody if I was born white. I felt before that I had the intelligence to be somebody . . . now I'm nothing.

Mrs. Belle Green
WE'RE THEIR ONES HERE IN THE WORLD 'TIL GOD COME

We're their ones here in the world 'til God come, but they don't like we colored people. All these here want out you is work. And they can get 'em— give us our three dollar a week. You not going to feed yourself with that. Outside of that, you can go.

Mrs. Janie Hunter
I CAN'T FIGURE IT OUT

You find people 'ssociate with Negro 'round here, Charleston is not their home. That is one thing I can't understand, because we have to do everything for them. I was working for my lady for three years. I raise her baby. Mostly all these people have a maid or baby-sitter. You can't 'ssociate with 'em and then people want you to cook their food and take care their children. I can't figure it out.

Mr. William Saunders

THEY DON'T WANT TO GET OUT ON A LIMB

I believe, in my honest opinion, that there's a whole lot of white people on this island that's not bad at all. And I think they would like to see everybody happy, but they don't want to get out on a limb from their own people, be called "nigger-lovers" or any other stories that the people can dream up for them.

I knew a white guy and we sat around and was drinking beer and talking and he was saying that he was with the Negroes in most of the things that they wanted and he believed that most of the things they wanted was right. He said he has never done nothing to hurt the Negroes. I told him that I felt like he hadn't done anything to help the Negroes either because he just sat back and was sort of looking out for his personal self, instead of saying to his friends, when they have gatherings and the question comes up, "I don't believe that we are right in what we are doing. I believe that everybody should have a chance."

I think seriously that we got a whole lot of Negroes that are hurting us more than the whites, by acting content—like the maids in the house. Any time the madam would say something to them, they would smile even though within themselves they were unhappy. But this is what was expected of them and so this is what they're doing. They have been conditioned to this. They are not frank and not honest with themselves or the people they deal with. I believe this is one of the things that's hurting us because then the white man feel that he could always push you back, because you're just that way; you're not going to stand up to nothing.

Mr. William Saunders

ALL WOULD BE GETTING EQUAL EDUCATION

As far as Johns Island is concerned, we got a long way to go. I believe sincerely that there will have to be something that happens real bad to change the situation here. We've coexisted all these years. We have accepted this, and the white man have accepted it. Very seldom do we have to come together on any major thing. So in this respect we could make it if we could keep on going like that, but we can't. Because we have gotten to the place now that my kids are not wanting what I wanted, or *thought* I wanted.

Nobody has applied yet to go to the white high school. But I think when it come right down to it, it's gonna be accepted. Actually Johns Island is real poor and I don't think nobody could afford for money to be cut off from the schools. The superintendent of the schools told me that if the schools were closed, the Negroes would suffer more than the whites. I don't believe this, and I don't believe that he believes it, because actually to me then we all would be getting equal education—nobody gets none.

Miss Carol Bligen
I KNOW BE TROUBLE

If they integrated Haut Gap School, be trouble. I know be trouble, 'cause I don't like nobody to tease me. If one of them come and tease me, first thing I do, I going fight.

Mr. William Saunders
INTIMIDATION HAS BEEN BAD

The whites and the Negroes on this island haven't gotten involved in violence. But the intimidation, I think, has been bad as far as the white is concerned. Like making a person feel like he might not have a job tomorrow. This is something that bothers the Negroes a whole lot. Although it never bothered me because I feel like anybody that works me, he's working me because he's making some money off me, he's not working me because he likes me. He's working me because I'm a good worker and he needs me. And I believe that we all need each other—without the whites the Negro couldn't make it; and I believe without the Negroes the whites couldn't make it.

They've used the migrant workers in this intimidation. When I first knew about the migrant workers, they were really, really treated bad. They had no place to stay when they came here, and they were always treated bad. But since the integration movement has started here on the island, I think the white farmers have really gone for the migrant workers because they know that the migrant laborers really don't stand for nothing. They're just somebody to work.

Most of them, I've found out, have been in trouble before. They had trouble somewhere, or they couldn't make it at home, or something like that, and that's how come they become migrant laborers. So the white farmers figure, "Here's a chance for us to use the Negroes without the Negroes really being able to do anything about it. We don't have to worry about them getting an education. All they want to do is get our crops out, and then we can sort of hurt the Negroes here on the island by doing it this way."

The biggest farmer here, during the last season, he was working the migrant laborers three days and the regular Negroes on the island two days a week. So this is something where the Negroes used to look forward to making during the summertime eighty or ninety dollars a week, it be cut down to thirty-five or forty dollars a week.

This is to try to keep the Negroes from participating in things. It doesn't matter whether he or she has been participating or not, he's automatically placed in this category. Two farmers came by the Progressive Club last year during the workshops there and acted like they were taking down license numbers. Nobody knows if they were actually taking down the numbers or not; they never published them, but this really scared a lot of Negroes and they wouldn't even want to bring their cars around.

Rev. G. C. Brown
WE GOT ALONG

The Negroes have been afraid to trust the white. They feel he isn't wanting them to begin with, and the white men feel that they are superior. That's what we have on this island.

There has never been any race problem since I've been here. By race problem I mean there hasn't been any violence. We got along. The Negroes just used to take things as accepted course. They been resigned to their fate, most of them, and satisfied with that.

You can tell the difference in the whites' attitude since 1954. They weren't quite as friendly, some of 'em, as they had been, because they thought there was going to be a rushing into the white schools, and they didn't want that. But I don't think they have to fear about that. Nobody's ever tried to go there.

It's just a matter of time until they are going to accept integration. Well, I don't know about Johns Island. I won't say that here because, you see, people accept according to their education, I believe. The more a man knows, the more intelligent he becomes of worldly affairs. But now this island here is going to be a long time, I think.

The newspaper see a relation between the two races, they make that white man a Communist. Infiltration! Any time relationship between Negroes and whites, always be somebody tag 'em as a Communist. That's one of the policies of this Southland you'll find. They don't have anything else to say, they just say that. Just like Martin Luther King. They say he's a Communist and that's not true. Just a man trying to get what belongs to him.

Mr. Esau Jenkins
WE NEED TO MAKE FRIENDS

I have a white friend and we usually be frank with each other. He ask me, "Don't you think that the Negro want integration because they want to marry white women?"

I laughed. I said, "Are you kidding? You ever know any garden that's pretty without having a variety of flowers?" I said, "If you have all black flowers or all white flowers you don't have much of a garden, but if you have all kinds of flowers it looks pretty. Now Negroes can choose from almost white to the very black and different shades between, and then he's just wanting to have integration to marry a white woman?"

Years ago the Negroes on this island were skeptical of a white person if he show as if he want a friendship with them or help them, because only thing they know about the white folks is go out and work for them and they treat them as animal, and that's all. That's the kind of relationship they call good—to go out and do what they want done and then go home. Years ago, Negroes have never seen a white person come around, no more than if they come out to the house to ask them to work. They wouldn't even much come in, and the Negroes couldn't even go in the white folks house regardless of how much they work. But now things are changing a little bit.

Some time ago I went to a white home here, and I rung the bell, and to my surprise, the man invited me into the kitchen. We began to talk together, and the white girl came and peeped through the door to see who the daddy was talking to. And she went back to the mother and I heard the mother say, "Who is that?" and the girl say, "Mr. Jenkins." I was surprised she had said that. I just want to know what the mother thought when a white girl calling a Negro *Mister* Jenkins. That was a surprise to me. But we talk in a friendly manner 'til I ready to leave.

And I think it is because of these white persons who have come here, who have stayed with me lots of times, we have gone around together, we have sung together, we have prayed together, we have eaten together. And I think some of the white folks here are being ashamed of themselves just now. They can see the handwriting on the wall. We need to make friends.

You can see a change in the most of them. Not too many have come out openly and invited me in their home and sit with them as these one or two. The white magistrate has invited me in his home. We sat to the table together and discussed things on the island and the betterment of Negroes, and some white farmers have call me and we begin to talk. Not in the masses, but you can see the feeling, and they respect you much better. It's not the kind of relationship they were calling good relations some years ago, that you go out and do what I tell you to do and then go home.

Mr. William Saunders

FREEDOM IS WORSE

Really to me, freedom is worse in New York than it is on Johns Island. Because on Johns Island the white people are honest in letting you know that they don't want you to associate with them. In New York, if we go to a hotel and want a room, there's no segregation, they just ain't got no rooms.

Mrs. Mary Pinckney

DOWN ON ME

Chorus

Down on ___ me, ___ Lord, ___ down on ___ me ___

Oh, well, ___ my ___ Lord, ___ Seem like ev' - ry - bo - dy in this

whole ___ wide world ___ Is down on me. ___

Verse

Won - der what Sa - tan is ___ growl - in' a - bout ___

Chained in Hell ___ and he can't ___ get ___ out ___

Seem like ev' - ry - bo - dy in this whole ___ wide world ___ is ___ down on me. ___

I been buked and I been scorned,
I been talked about sure as you're born.
Seem like everybody in this whole wide world
   Is down on me.

When I get to Heaven going to sing and shout,
Nobody there going to put me out.
Seem like everybody in this whole wide world
   Is down on me.

You can talk about me just as you please;
The more you talk the more I'll bend my knees.
Seem like everybody in this whole wide world
   Is down on me.

One of these days and it won't be long,
You go look for me and I'll be gone.
Seem like everybody in this whole wide world
   Is down on me.

(**Chorus**)
Down on me, Lord, down on me.
Oh, well, my Lord, seem like everybody in this whole wide world
   Is down on me.

155

RIGHT TO THE TREE OF LIFE?

PROGRESS ON JOHNS ISLAND

Esau Jenkins

Rev. G. C. Brown

THE STRUGGLE HAS COME WITH ESAU

He's a self-made man—what you call pulling up by your own boot-straps. Everybody here live practically on the same level, but Esau is in a class all by himself.

When we first came to Johns Island in '36 I saw there was a future for Esau. He used to come to me for night teaching. I taught him, right here in my house, to continue his English and grammar and reading. Then, when he stopped coming here, he went to night school at Burke in the city and developed and increased his knowledge.

There's not another one here like him. I knew his father. He belonged to this church, but his father was not that type of person. He was the kind of "you doing too much, Esau . . . ." You know.

We have a civic organization here on Johns Island and Esau is the president. He's tried to let other people take over, but we elect somebody, he serve maybe three months and give it up, and Esau just have to take it back over again. That's why he's stayed in office so long. Others become discouraged and quit. But he hasn't ever become discouraged. He just work on through.

There's always two groups when somebody like Esau builds himself up—one that appreciates and another that doesn't think too well of it. I think now most everybody sees what he's done and I don't think he has much opposition. But he had opposition to begin with—opposition from his own people. They went to the white people, and they gave him hard knocks, but he kept right on persisting; didn't never stop. But now they see he's going to make it anyway, so they just decided to let him off.

One reason people criticized Esau so much, they afraid he going too fast. They been resigned to their fate most of them, and satisfied with that. The struggle has come with Esau. Esau has advocated justice, and don't be satisfied until you get justice.

There's been a great awakening through television and through the news media. They all begin to know now that we've been treated wrong for a long time. They are more conscious of that every day now. And you'll find a greater desire on the part of the individual to get some of the good things of life. But now, people still don't help Esau as much as they should. The prophet is without honor in his own country.

Mr. Esau Jenkins
AM I MY BROTHER'S KEEPER?

Long years ago I ask myself a question, Am I my brother's keeper? And the answer that I got was, You are. So then I decided to myself, since I'm no better than anybody, I don't feel I'm any worse than anybody. I decided to do anything I can to help people in order to help myself.

I have two question asked to me by other people. The first question was, how was I able to educate five children and live, born and raised on Johns Island—have never taught a school in my life, have never work for the government—and they all have made good grades in school, and they have been very mannerable to everybody. The way you raise your children, you can make 'em be lovable in this world, or you make 'em be hated by people, so it's your responsibility. Since God is kind enough to give you a child, then you ought to raise 'em the way he should go.

Then a man came to me and ask me, said, "Look, I notice them buses you have look so nice, and I understand you have sent all your children to school and you have gotten some property you own and doing some business. Where do you buy your hoodo root from?"

Now you know that's silly. Hoodoo business. That's the thing that make people poor, because they believe in root. So I said to him (I didn't have the answer right away because I might have said something bad to him), but I said, "Look friend, where I got my root from, it only takes obedience and a simple mind to go home and go into your closet and get on your knees and ask God for what you want."

And I tell you one thing: every progress that I have made in life, it came to me while I was doing some good for somebody.

Mr. Esau Jenkins

THEY PAINTED IT BLACK

I haven't gotten any further than the fourth grade in grammar school here. I had to work, and because of that I had to leave school. And then too, the school we had here wasn't encouraging to go to. We had around fifty children and one teacher with a one-door school.

And beside that, they painted it black, that we could be identified as to who go to the school. It discouraged me when I got some pride. I left school and went to Charleston and started working on a boat. But I still was serious about getting my education. I know I couldn't have done anything out of a fourth-grade education.

Then I got married some years later and find out that I have a great responsibility, and I know that my education was limited. So I decided that I would work and go to school at the same time. I went four years more, which help me to transact my own business, and now I'm happy to say that

160

I was able to have my children educated. One son is a captain in the Army, one a navigator in the Air Force, two daughters are teaching, one son is a professor of music.

And now there are other folks on this island being encouraged to send their children to get a higher education. We know that some day in the near future Johns Island will be a better place to live.

Rev. G. C. Brown
ESAU STARTED THE MOVEMENT, WITH HIS OWN CHILDREN IN A LITTLE TRUCK

When I came here thirty years ago, there was no chance for any schooling beyond the fifth and sixth grade. Esau started the movement by going into Charleston, with his own children in a little truck, taking them to Burke High School.

Then the County eventually consented to pay the tuition at Burke for all who graduated the eighth grade here. And the load kept increasing as the nine little schools on the island educated a group every spring. So they decided it would be better to go ahead and build a school over here with the people, and consolidate rather than to pay this tremendous tuition cost and transportation to Charleston. And that's how Haut Gap High School came to be here.

Esau started it. He's the originator of it. They might not give him credit for getting that school built, but I know 'cause I was here.

Mr. Esau Jenkins
IT'S GOOD TO DO YOUR OWN FIGURING

I shall never forget those days when I have worked long on the farm—for fifty cents a day—plowed, lined out straight rows to spread fertilizer in, and come back and put the potatoes in the trench and cover it up.

At that time I was about eighteen or twenty years old. I married when I was seventeen, and because I felt like that wasn't any kind of money to support a family with, I left and went to work somewhat for myself.

My father was a farmer and a carpenter. He was doing carpenter work when he was much younger, and he tried to teach me how to do it. I worked with him for a while, but I didn't like carpenter work too well. I imagine I was a little bit lazy, that kind of thing. But my father was very smart in carpentry. He built a house in a few days if you just give him the material. But then as he got older he turned more to farming.

My father was a man believe in whatever the white folks said. He didn't want to hurt them a bit. I know after I start farming with him, one day we went to carry some cotton to sell. The white man who figured what the cotton come to, he gave us a certain price. I started to figure mine.

Daddy told me, "Don't do that. The white folks never like that, Son."

I say, "Well, I'm not figuring for the white folks at this point, I'm figuring for my own benefit."

Well, he never figured, but I figured mine. Unfortunately, mine was wrong when the white man figured, but I wouldn't take it. I waited until everybody got the money, including my daddy, and I went to him. "According to what you paid me, my money didn't come to what it should come to for the amount of cotton I had."

So he said, "Well, let me see." Sure enough, he found out that he made a mistake.

But now if I said that before everybody, there might have been everybody who was there think that his own was wrong too. And everything might have been, but I *know* mine was wrong. And I certainly glad I was able to figure.

I told my daddy, say "Now Daddy, you see I don't know how long this man doing it, but this figuring was wrong, and I don't know how many other person was wrong, but I didn't say it because I was afraid that everybody would say the same thing, and then he would blame me for it. But can't you see it's good to do your own figuring?"

Of course, I convince him at that time, but he never would do it.

Mr. Esau Jenkins
THEN I NOTICE THE GREEKS

I planted cotton for about four, five years—my father and I together. It takes one whole year to harvest cotton. Then my mind tell me to start with vegetables. Then most of the people start on vegetable farming—truck crop farming, where you can plant three vegetables a year, no doubt four. That's what prompt me to buy a truck.

Then I notice as I go into the city to sell my vegetables, most of the stores are operated by Greeks. They buy all kind of vegetables. So I thought the best thing for me to do then is to try to learn the Greeks' language. I could sell more stuff and help me to do more business and help my family better. So I went and took Greek. I took Greek for about a year and a half or two, and I was able to understand the Greek language in everyday speaking in business, and that helped me to go on. That is the thing that helped me to educate most of my children.

Mr. Esau Jenkins
HERE'S A MAN BEING SHOT FOR A DOG

Two evil things that happened motivated me to get involved in my work on Johns Island. In September of 1938 two Negroes were riding in a truck. A dog ran out of a gate. The man driving tried to avoid it, but he couldn't, he hit the dog and killed it. The dog's owner, a white man (he wasn't a native of Johns Island, but had come here to live), jumped in his own car, and he carried a shotgun and ran this man down.

The fellow who wasn't driving tried to plead with him, ask him not to shoot him because he didn't mean to run over this dog, but he shot this fellow dead.

The family got a white lawyer from Charleston to try to bring that case in the court, and from 1938 until this present time, nobody heard any more of that case.

Well, that's something that I felt like people who have good will and think about decency and human dignity should do something about.

Then in the early '40s a white man, Mr. Malone, move from Mississippi onto Johns Island. He was sixty years old, his wife was twenty. They had a female dog and as a rule at certain times of the year, several dogs will go around these homes with female dogs. For some reason her dog was across the street one morning at a Negro man's home. She heard her dog's voice hollering as if somebody was beating the dog, and she went over and asked this Negro man by the name of Sammy Grant if he put his dog on her dog.

He said, "No, I didn't."

She said, "Yes, you did."

And he said, "Whoever said I put my dog on your dog tell a damn lie."

So she went back home, and we don't know what she told her husband.

Every morning Mr. Malone caught a truck about seven o'clock to go to work. The next morning, when the truck came by, he stopped it and called to Sammy Grant. By the time Sammy came around by the tail of the truck, Mr. Malone shot him right there. He was so close, and with a 12-gauge gun, this boy bled a lot.

The man who owned the truck stop a car and rush him to the hospital. By the time he got there, he had bled out the blood that would keep him alive, and the doctor asked this man to rush out and get some blood right away, 'less he was going to die.

The man came down to the city market where people sell the vegetables to find the guardian of this boy or the mother to try to get some blood, or try to get some money to buy blood for him. She said she didn't have any money. Everybody was standing around saying it was wrong, he should not have been shot. But I said, "Are you trying to help this boy? You can't listen to people say it's wrong. If they feel sorry for the boy they'll go down and give him blood."

I said, "Wait a minute, I'll get two of my brother-in-laws and I will go down and give him blood." So we went down. I gave the first pint and my two brother-in-laws gave the other two pints and save his life.

I ask him to tell me the truth what happened. I said to him, "Sammy, just as I gave you my blood to save your life, I will spend every dime and make sacrifice for you to help bring this thing to justice through the court." And he told me just what I've said.

So I went on Broad Street and hired a lawyer. He ask me to find a hundred dollars because he said he have to hire a stenographer to carry to Johns Island. The magistrate might not stick to the word he said in the court, so he need somebody to keep a record.

For a long time we heard nothing about the case. Finally I called up this lawyer and ask him what's wrong. I fussed at him a long time. Then we heard from the other man's lawyer that he wanted to make some kind of deal with Sammy. And we went and met with this lawyer.

I told him, "Mr. Malone shot Sammy with malice of forethought. Now I realize that it's a bad thing to call a woman a liar, but I don't think a man should be shot down for calling somebody a liar."

I said, "You know we have had one man shot dead over a dog and nothing came of it. The family paid a white lawyer to look out for the family and bring this thing to trial and nobody heard anything from it yet. Here's another man being shot for a dog. Now this is bad for race relations."

I told him if he were to come to Johns Island, with one man shot outright and another shot and left for dead, he might not be safe—and he could be ever so right, but because of the things that happened, Negroes began to get malice in their heart for white folks. We can't afford to let things like that go on. We, as people who know better, should make it better and make race relations better.

So he decided to pay us what Sammy had lost. He said that he hadn't felt like he was going to lose the case, but if he had won the case in court and then heard what I had just told him afterward, he never would have felt himself justified.

These are the things, then, that motivated me to organize in 1949 a progressive movement, that we could help the people to be better citizens, give them a chance to get a better education, and know how to reason and look out for themselves, and take more part in political action.

Mrs. Janie Hunter and
the Moving Star Hall congregation

YOU GOT TO MOVE

I got to move,____ we got_ to move,_____ We got to move,_____ we got to move,_____ Oh, when the Lord,____ Lord get read - y, you got to move. Oh, _____

ALTERNATE VERSION

You may be rich, you may be poor,_____ You may be high,_____ you may be low, _____ But when the Lord_____ get read - y, _____ you got to move. Oh,

My brother move, my brother move,
My brother move, my brother move.
Oh, when the Lord get ready, you got to move.

O sometime I'm up, sometime I'm down,
Sometime I'm almost to the ground.
Oh, when the Lord get ready, you got to move.

Oh we got to move, we got to move,
We got to move, we got to move.
When the Lord, Lord get ready, you got to move.

Mr. Esau Jenkins

"MR. JENKINS, I WOULD LIKE VERY MUCH TO BECOME A REGISTERED CITIZEN."

On Johns Island, in the year of 1948, I saw the condition of the people who had been working on the plantations for many years. And I knew that we were not able to do the things that would need to be done unless we could get people registered citizens.

I operated a bus from Johns Island to Charleston carrying people to their jobs. So I decided to get a group in the bus in the mornings and teach them how to read the part of the Constitution that we have to read before we are able to become registered citizens.

One of these mornings I was teaching the group to read the Constitution, a woman by the name of Alice Wine said to me, "Mr. Jenkins, I would like very much to become a registered citizen, but I cannot read this Constitution because I did not get but just so far in school, and I cannot pronounce these words. But if you are willing to help me, I will show you that I would be one that would be willing to vote in every election."

So I decided to pay more attention to her, and I helped her at more times than I do the regular times when we have school in the bus, to get her prepared to register.

Mrs. Alice Wine

EVERYBODY READ AND GET A PAPER

I come around to registering through Mr. Esau Jenkins. I used to ride his bus, and he said, "I want to carry you down to register." I said, "I can't read those hard thing yet," and he get the book and he start to learn me.

He start to help me read and when I get to them hard words I feel like jump it. My tongue so heavy until I couldn't pronounce the words, you know. But he said to me, "No, the hard word is the things for you to learn." And so me and them girls (and some of the girls could read 'em—dum-de-dum-dum-dum—right on through, right on through, but I couldn't do it), we tried 'em.

Then he take we up to a registration board on Society Street, and we get in line. Everybody read and get a paper, read and get a paper. And I be in line next to this girl, and she read and she stammer. And then the man put me for read, and I read those things just like I been know 'em. And I didn't know them things, I swear!

Mr. Jenkins figure I going fail. He been right outside there on the corner for listen. And when I come out he said, "Miss Wine, you get it?" I say, "Yes, sir." Say, "Well, sir!" I say, "I thought I couldn't read them hard thing." Them thing was *too* hard!

Mr. Esau Jenkins

EVERYBODY IS JUBILANT FOR THE HIGHLANDER FOLK SCHOOL

The Negroes outnumber the white here 'round about two and a third to one. The potential voting strength for Negroes is about two thousand against around one thousand white, if we could get them all registered. They have been doing it much faster now, because I know the last ten years before the new registration started, it took us ten years to get seventy-five or a hundred person registered, and then starting back in 1957–1958 it got better. Since then we put nearly four hundred people on the books. They are civic-minded now, and they want to take part in it. I think so much progress has been made in the last few years due to the citizenship school that was started here by the Highlander Folk School.

I first attended Highlander in 1954. They asked each individual to give the immediate problem in his locality. My immediate problem was adult education, because so many person were here who couldn't read and write and I know this condition, because I would have been almost in the same condition if I didn't go back to school. So I asked the Highlander Folk School officials if it were possible to help us set up night schools for these people to help them become better citizens.

They said if I could find a place, could find a teacher, they could help take care of the expenses. So they did. And that was very, very important to helping us to get as many persons registered on this island.

And then people on Wadmalaw and Edisto Islands found out later the reason Johns Island was so successful in registering Negroes. They ask me if it's possible to help them to get an adult school. So the next year when I went to Highlander, when it comes time for immediate problem again, I brought in Wadmalaw and Edisto, and they again say they will help if I could find a place and the teachers. I found the place, and today Wadmalaw registered more Negroes than ever registered in the history of Wadmalaw. In the 1964 election Wadmalaw had about two hundred Negro votes for Johnson. Most of the white folks were voting for Goldwater, but Negroes voted enough to hold it in the Democratic column. That's the only area in Charleston County that went for Johnson.

The same thing is happening on Edisto and all over the county. In 1954 in the county there were 'round about five or six thousand Negroes registered. In 1964 almost fourteen thousand. So everybody is jubilant for the Highlander Folk School, who have helped them to see the light.

Mr. Esau Jenkins
KNOWING HOW TO PLAY THE GAME

We had gotten quite a few people registered through that adult citizenship school, but they did not have the political education or understanding of voting. So we decided to teach them what the ballot means. I started what we called the "second step" political education school, because the people who registered to vote would vote because we told them to vote.

There were many persons who did not know how many men in the House of Representatives; why Charleston County has eleven in the House; how many men in the Senate; how many congressional districts we have in South Carolina; who are the men elected and sent to Washington to represent these two districts. We feel that if these people know about these things, they will be more interested in voting, and they will help others.

As you know as well as I do, that if a person doesn't know a football game, a basketball game, neither a baseball game, he hears other people laugh and sees how other persons play, but he doesn't know *who* plays well, because he doesn't know the game.

The same thing goes with some of the people who don't know anything about political action, so we felt like it was our responsibility to teach those people and have them well-informed.

Along with political education, we have taught a good many persons how to sign checks, fill out money orders, how to crochet, how to sew, how to fill out blanks for their drivers' licenses. I think it was a great success.

Then after I was elected President of the Citizens' Committee of Charleston and Charleston County, I set up what we call a voter registration and information center, to which place people will come in for information. Whatever information they need, they come to this center.

Mr. Esau Jenkins
"MAN, ESAU JENKINS' NAME ON THE VOTING MACHINE!"

Then I ran for the school trusteeship on this island. I ran knowing that I wouldn't have won unless a miracle had been done. They had three white persons to run. I made four. And I came out third, so I got more votes than one of the white candidates. That scared some of the white folks here, and the man who is on the county council decided that they would change voting for trustees on the school board. They would have it be appointed because Johns Island strength was growing too much.

The reason why I ran is because I wanted the Negroes to know that it is their privilege to go into any office they're qualified to handle. They are taxpayers and they have just as much right to run for public office as the white persons. I ran because some Negroes thought that if a Negro name ever was placed on a voting machine, that person would be killed. Or they thought that a Negro's name couldn't be placed on a voting machine.

And so I ran and my name was placed in alphabetical order and they saw it. And when one of the guys went in and saw my name, he went and told the rest, say, "Man, Esau Jenkins' name on that voting machine," says, "You better go on down there and vote." And that year we had about ninety-nine percent of the Negroes who registered vote. Encourage them ever since to vote.

Mr. Esau Jenkins
WE'RE NOT FOR SALE

After we got started and the Negroes started registering, then a bribe was made to me. They sent someone to offer me whatever I want if I would stop teaching Negroes to register and vote and go along with the white folks. Well, I didn't accept it.

My argument at that time was that we need a high school on Johns Island and we need to get our children off their feet who are walking ten miles per day to try to get an education. They walk in the rain, in the cold, and the sleet and we believe it cause a health hazard. So I told this man who offered me the money, "We're not for sale, and we're only going to support people who are willing to see to it that our children will get a high school, plus transportation to take them to and from school."

The white kids were riding in school buses, and the buses were warm when they got into it. When they got to the school, the schools were warm. Yet our children had to walk between eight and ten miles per day, go to a cold school with no heat. The teachers that teach the school, they live in Charleston—fifteen or eighteen miles away—and the children have to stand outside until the teachers come. Then when the teachers come, if they didn't have any wood, they got to go out in back of the school and get wood to make up the fire. Whether it raining, whether it cold, whether it snowing, those children have to walk there, and after they got the fire started, it being so cold, I don't think they could concentrate so well. And beside that they

have forty to fifty children to one teacher, and have to carry 'em from scratch to seventh grade.

So we know that was a terrible condition, and that's the condition that I want to try to eliminate. And that's my reason for not taking this bribe. I know that we wouldn't have gotten anywhere, not as long as I was willing to take bribe and go along with the white folks. I had made some enemy by not taking the bribe. I had made some of my people afraid of me because I kept on fighting for the Negroes' right. But I didn't stop.

The white folks cut off this one big plantation that I used to haul to, as I had three buses and two trucks. Sometimes I make sixty dollars, sixty to eighty dollars a day, with three or four vehicle—twenty dollars for each one —to carry the people there. They cut that off, but I wouldn't stop. I keep on driving and keep on fighting.

Since we have gotten the high school, now we have had quite a few children graduated from the high school here on the island. Since then we have been able to get this consolidated grammar school, and we have buses.

Mr. Esau Jenkins
WE DIDN'T HAVE A CHANCE
WHEN WE GO INTO COURT

I'll tell you another way voting was able to help us. I could remember not too long ago, we didn't have a chance when we go into court. I remember a day I was riding with a man coming to Johns Island from Charleston, and a white person ran into the back of his truck. When we stop to find out what happen to the person, the law took side with the person who ran into the back of his truck, and he had to go to court.

We all thought that the judge would say, "Well, somebody ran into the back of the truck, certainly seem like that person is wrong." Unfortunately, he said that the colored man was wrong. He didn't have a chance in the court. But we decided to change that thing by getting people to see the importance of citizenship, registration and voting.

We got them to be interested in organizing what we call the Progressive Club. I emphasize the word "progressive" which mean look upward, do something better. And in this club we told them that if you're not registered to start with, you're going to have to *become* a registered citizen if you join. And we ask every individual to pay twenty-five cent per month. For what? Just in case when you go into these unjust courts, your money pools and somebody'll stand the bonds, or pay the fine. Now things are changed. The time would come when this same magistrate who have never listened to Negroes would need their vote.

One year when he ran for the third time, the white folks decided to vote against him—not all the white folks, just about fifty percent of them. And he was thinking about dropping out of the election. He came to me and ask, "What can you all do? I understand that the white folks is against me because in the court sometime ago I was little bit lenience with Negro."

So I told him if he would promise that he would treat Negroes better, make them realize that they are human being when they come into the court, not charge them for everything or just assume that they are wrong, but just give them what belongs to them—if they are right, let them know they are right—I said, "We will vote for you. We got a few Negroes voting. If you got fifty percent of your people, the rest of the Negroes certainly would turn the tide."

And when that night came, he won by the many Negroes had registration certificate. That change the situation. That magistrate now, whenever our people go into the court, he is very frank and fair with us. And so for that reason, we felt like the more we could get people registered, the better it would be.

Mrs. Alice Wine
HE IS A WONDERFUL CONQUEROR

We start the Progressive Club with about two or three hundred head of people in '48 or '49. We used to meet in Moving Star Hall every third Sunday and pay twenty-five cents a head. And after we done pay out for that piece of property we got now, we stop paying monthly dues.

There was a schoolhouse there, but we turn 'em into a store after we buy 'em. We put all our money together and open 'em up. And we call 'em Progressive Club. We been growing and growing. We is still in debt, but we are going on. And Mr. Jenkins, he is so good, he is so kind, so soft-hearted, he don't care what the people said, but he going on. He is a wonderful conqueror, I tell you that.

And John Smalls, he just stick and stand right there as a sale-man. Sell in the store. He is the head of buying for the store. Bill Saunders is the Manager of the store. And I am the Treasurer. Mr. Jenkins is the President. So we stick and stand, thick and thin, right there.

I think this the best place on Johns Island. I say to myself, "is a Christian place" because the good Lord help us so far in all these years. We ain't had no bad quarrels yet. 'Cause they always divide a row. I not say no row don't be there. They be there. But if they know, Esau or John, they will divide the row. They will ask them nicely to quit. Or they put them out. We never had nobody hurt one another yet.

Mr. Esau Jenkins
NOW WE CALL IT SEA ISLAND CENTER

The Progressive Club grew a little bit. We finished paying for the old building. Then after we have taken out what it takes to run the store for the year, each member (thirteen people) gets a dividend. The first year it was twenty-five dollars. Next year each person got thirty dollars. I felt like it was some motivation for all of them to find out that we are now getting something back.

And then I said to them that since this building was bought old and is about to outlive its usefulness, that we need to build something that will be serviceable to not only this community, but for the whole sea islands. I thought that a place large enough for basketball and other games and workshops would be something that could bring in other people to give ideas what could be done for the community and other communities. I suggested to them that this ought to be done. I felt like if we got together and work heartily together, cooperatively together, that it could be done.

We have one or two person oppose my idea about a huge building like that, for fear that we wouldn't be able to pay for the thing, or that we wouldn't even be able to get it built to start with. One of the members stated that he hoped he could live long enough to see one side of the wall go up. When I was told that, I said maybe he didn't feel he have long to live. I guess he was surprised to see it go up.

One member couldn't believe that Negroes could get together and pool their money and buy something and get along all right. It took me ten years to convince him. He told somebody that when I first started the Progressive Club he thought I was looking out for Esau Jenkins and the family. This person told me, "But I found out when you went and bought that place. The money was loaned to you, and you put all as many names as possible on

the deed, and let them run it, and just check with them once a month, so they believe you meant good for them. And now I have all the confidence in you." Evidently that's the reason why it took me ten years to make him realize we can get along together.

The whole entire group work faithfully with me now. I think we are doing very well because of the fact that we are working together. And more people are using the place now. They see the need for it.

They didn't have any place to go on this island for recreation. That's one reason we built this, and then call it "sea island" center instead of community center, because we serve James Island, Johns Island and Wadmalaw. Unless they play in somebody's yard, there's not a place where they can have a proper game on any one of these islands.

Our school doesn't have a gym, probably won't ever have one. In October of this year the basketball teachers came down to the Progressive

Club and asked us to let them play basketball there. They'd been playing outside during this basketball season, and they'd been getting beat eighty-something to twenty.

Last night we had the school come in and they had a talent show, and had a record hop behind it, and I understand about two hundred head or more were there. Then we started a Boy Scout here. We are interested in getting the boys because we feel like it would be a good thing for young boys to be a better citizen. They are planning to have their programs at the Club.

Then we have a young citizenship group that we organized. It concerns itself with race relations and voter registration or everything that goes to make the human being happy. They got a volume of encyclopedia to study a variety of words that they might have a vocabulary large enough to answer questions. And they feel happy about it, because that's one of the things kept them from running up and down the street and have nothing else to do.

I stated before that we emphasize the word "progressive." If we are going to be progressive on this island, we still have a lot to do.

Mr. Esau Jenkins
THOSE TYPEWRITER CAME FALLING DOWN
IN THE SCHOOL, OVERNIGHT

We need better equipment and better instruction in our schools to make our children better able to compete with other children. I felt there are so many Negroes whose children wouldn't be college material, and so many Negroes' income wouldn't allow them to send their children to college. If a child goes to school and just take up home economics and some agriculture, they wouldn't able to use it when they come out, and they be just as bad or worse off than a child who hasn't gone to high school who will go on the farm and work and never think about it.

The child who had been through high school feel bad scrubbing somebody's floor or working on the farm—much worse than the child who never had any training. So my suggestion was that the school give shorthand and typing.

I told Robert Johnson, a man who is very energetic in doing things, to go to the Haut Gap School and ask the principal if it be possible to get in some typewriters and give shorthand and typing, that our girls who would want to be secretary and can't go to college would come out and know how to do something. They could take dictation and maybe could be hired in some of these lawyers' offices.

The principal told him that the boys and girls there don't have the aptitude for that kind of thing. In fact he said that on the national average the boys and girls who finish Haut Gap School are no more than about tenth grade scholars. So Mr. Johnson say, "I surprise to hear you say that, because it seem you ought to try to correct that kind of thing, if it be true."

The principal sent Mr. Johnson to the man who is the supervisor over the schools here on Johns Island. The supervisor told him that the typewriters would cost a lot of money. If he insist that his daughter or some other girls take typing and shorthand, they could go to the Negro high school on James Island. Mr. Johnson contention was that that would be too far away.

Then I found out one day that the white high school on Johns Island had typing and shorthand. A white man came to my restaurant to fix the cigarette machine and said to me, "Esau, I congratulate you for sending your children to college." He said, "I couldn't send my daughter, but she has a good job. She works for one of the lawyers downtown."

I ask him, "Where did your daughter get her training?"

He said, "St. John's High."

I said, "St. John's High doesn't teach shorthand and typing."

He said, "Oh, yes it does. That's where my daughter learned and she's making good now."

Well that burn me a little bit when he told me that, so I brought it up that Sunday in the PTA, and I talk a long time about it. I told the principal and the teachers, "This is our children being hurt. I went all out for a high school here on Johns Island—I guess a lot of people were afraid to walk with me, some of my own race—because I was fighting white folks. Yet I was fighting that our tax money would be beneficial to our children. Now we need typewriters here. If we don't get it, certainly I'll try to find anybody who I know, as many as I know, to send to St. John's High School."

Well, I know they didn't want the Negroes to come there at that time, because you know this thing hadn't gotten full under way yet about integration. But we could make some trouble.

So I was told that Monday morning somebody rush to the superintendent's office and said, "You know, Esau talk a lot down there yesterday, and that crazy Negro say he'll send somebody to St. John's High School." He say, "The best thing you better do, you better try to get them typewriters."

So those typewriter came falling down in the school, overnight just about. I don't think they got the person to teach shorthand yet. Some of the teachers said it seemed like I was against them. I tell them, "I wasn't against any of you, but I asked you not to get in the way. You're not going to stand in the way of our children's education. You got yours."

Mr. Esau Jenkins
I AM TRYING TO GET HELP THROUGH
THE WAR ON POVERTY

Because I feel there needs to be work here for our young people, and care for our children so their parents can also make a good wage, I am trying to get help through the War on Poverty.

I told the poverty committee that I am a native of Johns Island. I said that I have been working over the years trying to obliterate ignorance, to promote health, social, educational and civic welfare, and to combat juvenile delinquency and to secure a more rich and abundant life to ourselves and to our posterity. I told them that we have obligated ourselves and denied ourselves and begged and borrowed money to help build a center that our boys and girls and adults could have a place on the island where they can have games and workshops and where we have had some folk song festivals which have brought together people of both races.

Now our people are asking us to assist them in many areas in which we cannot give help unless we get some kind of grant. They are asking for day care for preschool children so that they do not have to keep older children home from school while the parents are out working. They are asking for classes which will help them to earn some kind of living here—sewing, crafts, adult remedial reading, music, some kinds of mechanical skills. They are asking for the creation of some jobs for children who have left school, and after-school jobs for school children.

These requests have come from parents who make from $600 to $2,000 a year and have from two to eight children in their homes.

If we receive the grant we have asked for, we can employ twelve or fourteen persons for the Progressive Club Sea Island Center's program—a director, assistant director, dietician, secretaries, teachers, assistants, and a janitor.

We promised the committee if they would give us this badly needed grant, which would help alleviate the cycle of poverty in this area, we are willing to do our part in seeing it become a reality.

Mr. William Saunders
WHEN YOU FINISH THIS HIGH SCHOOL, YOU AREN'T PREPARED FOR ANY JOB

Most of the kids that leave the island, I would say ninety percent of 'em go to New York. And to me, New York is about the worst place that any good youngster could go. They'll come back and tell you that they're living nice, everything is really nice. The young girls go away angels, have never had anything to do with a man, and they go away for about two years and come back with three babies. And a lot of the kids get to be addicts. Some of them do all right, come back driving big cars and really influencing the kids that are here to go away.

The kids that get college education, it might help them individually but it sure doesn't help this island. It seems like they forget from where they came, or what they've suffered through, and the help that the rest of the people need. And our schools don't offer what the kids need to go to college anyhow. Yet our kids will get out of school and won't come back home to try to help the kids to get what they really need to even go to college. You can be an A-student here on the island, which don't take very much, and go to college and be a C-student or even flunk out.

When you graduate from this high school you aren't prepared for any job, except farming. You can't borrow no money from the bank to start a farm of your own, so they just prepare you to work on a farm here. They now offer typing, but like my first cousin was an honor student at Haut Gap and her teacher told her that she was too smart to take typing and short-hand. She tried to get into this new Technical Educational Center here and she couldn't get in. So now she's in New York. I know she's an angel, but what's going to be her fate? We don't know. She wrote back home and told her daddy, "Please make sure my brothers and sisters (she got about six or seven) get shorthand and typing." So her daddy bought a typewriter and got everybody in the house typing now.

Rev. G. C. Brown
IF WE COULD ONLY KEEP OUR YOUNG PEOPLE HERE

If we could only keep our young people here, but now when they finish high school, most of 'em go. They don't stay here to help you develop things. They're looking for better wages—fact, they have to do that. There's nothing much for them to do here but cut cabbages or run a tractor, maybe drive a truck or do something in the field. And there's not much money in it for them.

They mostly go to New York and find jobs somehow or other—working as domestics or doing small factory work. Very few ever come back to live. They come back to visit about once a year. But they don't ever come back to live.

Mr. William Saunders
GOING TO NEW YORK IS AN ADVANTAGE AND A DISADVANTAGE

Most people think about their kids. It's so hard raising kids in New York. And it's so easy for kids to go bad there. So most of the kids are left here with the grandparents while the parents are in New York working, and when they get a certain age they think about it. And they rebel. They find something bad to do. They try to get back somehow at their parents.

Most of the people that go away from here leave their kids. If the wife and the husband are going to be working, they have nobody to care for the kids, so they leave them home. And the grandparents have gotten to a certain age, they raised their kids, and they're so much more lenient on their grandkids than they were on their own kids. So this is one of the real big problems, I think. The kids suffer.

I was born in New York. I was one of these babies that was shipped here—not even somebody bringing me, they used to put tags on you and just put you on the train and say where you're supposed to get off at. I was raised by my grandparents and actually when a grandparent raise a kid, there are two generations between, and there's so much less understanding there. Things that the parents would probably understand, the grandparents cannot understand. And this was my problem.

This is something that is still going on, and I think it's gonna be going on and on. And this is one of the things that the Negroes have really been suffering from—this grandparents raising the children and the children not getting actually what they need. I believe if a kid really wants something, like he wants music lessons or he wants to study farming, or anything, if they say that they *want* to do it, I think that somebody should be there to help them with it. So even if they fail, they can't say, "I didn't have the opportunity." I think he should have the right to try, and if he fails, he can't blame nobody but himself because he just couldn't make it.

But like me now, I can sit back and blame my grandparents and my parents for not being successful. I don't know, I just feel to me that I could have been somebody. And I got somebody to blame for not being somebody.

Kids here need an opportunity.

Going to New York is a disadvantage and an advantage. To live I think it's a disadvantage. Some things are lacking here, but the children have a home. So we don't have everything that we want for them. But they have their home, so all they need is to get along like everybody else—daily living.

And it really shouldn't be that hard. The pay here is less, but you don't have to pay rent, and the food is cheaper. They go to New York and then they come back here on their vacation and tell you how silly you are to be here. And what they bring here is a new car, but then you have a car and you have a house, so what is it they're bringing? They're making more but they're spending more. But yet you're here with your kids, and they aren't.

And really they miss everything about home up there. That's why you find Christmas times or holiday times they don't want to be in New York, they want to be home. They miss the atmosphere, the friendliness of the people. You can go to anybody's house, the people don't have no money in the bank, they don't have no money under their mattress, but they got a whole lot of food. I don't believe there's a house around here where they ain't got a whole lot of food, got a little moonshine to drink on the holidays.

A lot of my friends say if they could make even thirty dollars a week less than they make in New York they would come back home.

Mr. Esau Jenkins

OUT OF EGYPT I AM GOING TO CALL MY SONS

Now if anybody is happy, it ought to be Esau Jenkins, the person who is talking here to you. Why? Twelve years and some months ago in this community, I organized a club—what we call the Progressive Club.

You folks have helped me start as a man and form a group. You are selling groceries, you are selling gasoline. Besides that, some time the early part of this month you have paid out all your debt and yet left $175 to add to your store.

When I organized this Progressive Club, I could count the number of voters on my one hand, and I don't have but five fingers.

In twelve years you have caused this whole island to change. Today you got school buses running by your door and picking up your children, carrying them to a high school on Johns Island. Today you can say that my children will be educated—at least get a high school education on Johns Island.

Today you could say in the last election we built up our voting strength so high until the white men in Charleston have to ask us to be in the polls on Johns Island and Edisto and Wadmalaw. Negroes have helped work for the Democratic party.

Now you could not have said that twelve years ago because you didn't vote. You didn't have a school. But today you have children getting ready to compete with anybody's children, because of your cooperation.

My friends, I want you to help me that I may go on, come what may. There are any number of times that I have walked alone. There are a lot of people who are afraid, because if they be seen walking along with me, the white folks might say, "Well, he is one of these persons who are fighting me."

But share it with Esau Jenkins, and thank God that God has helped us. We made an achievement that we are not ashamed of. You don't know how much you have done, friends—how many people are talking about what you have done; how many people are reading about what you have done.

Together let us go—sisters, brothers, blacks, whites, yellows, whatnot. We are all God's people, so we got to go together. And friends, I think all over the world today, people who love freedom are saying this morning, "Out of Egypt I'm going to call my sons."

The Moving Star Hall congregation

AIN'T YOU GOT A RIGHT TO THE TREE OF LIFE?

LEADER: Tell my father,
   GROUP: Ain't you got a right,
LEADER: Tell my father,
   GROUP: Ain't you got a right,
LEADER: Tell my father,
   GROUP: Ain't you got a right,
ALL: Ain't you got a right to the tree of life?

Tell my children . . . etc.

Tell the world . . . etc.

Hey, Lord,
   Ain't you got a right,
Hey, Lord,
   Ain't you got a right,
Hey, Lord,
   Ain't you got a right,
Ain't you got a right to the tree of life?

188